AF254821

Picturing Gratitude

Picturing Gratitude

An Art Journey on the Wings of Life

Susan M. Simmons

Exceptional Resources, Inc.
Publishing
www.ExceptionalResources.com

The Journey

As each moment unfolds before me, it opens a doorway — an opportunity or a choice to form a new thought or stick to the previous one. I like "opportunity" better. It's motivating! Being stuck in a thought of the past is like being stuck at a giant traffic light in outer space, unable to continue around the sun on this great flight we call life. What an amazing gift, albeit a challenge, we were handed. We were never promised a perfect world. Life has ups and downs, and everything in between.

As each new experience occurs — whether it's just me being myself or seeing someone I love leave the planet — I remind myself that I am still here and I was given a life to live. I also love being here and plan to continue forward on my journey with enthusiasm.

Grief, as we all experience, comes in many forms: Loss of a job, a house, or loved ones — all in varying degrees. This is life, which isn't always fair. Grief is many things, but *easy* not one of them. Freedom, however, comes from within. I make conscious efforts daily to say one or many gratitudes out loud. I rejoice all of the good things, rather than complain about the things that are not good.

I'm not wise, nor do I have all the answers. I just know what works for me. A personal history is just that — personal. I do, however, offer a glimpse of my life through the emotional effects my paintings bring forth through the past five decades. They were and are reflections of all the facets of my life thus far — the ups *and* the downs.

As I continue each journey around the sun, I'm grateful for the little things, and satisfied knowing that I am able to be so.

Ooooo! I love this planet!

Forever Who We Are

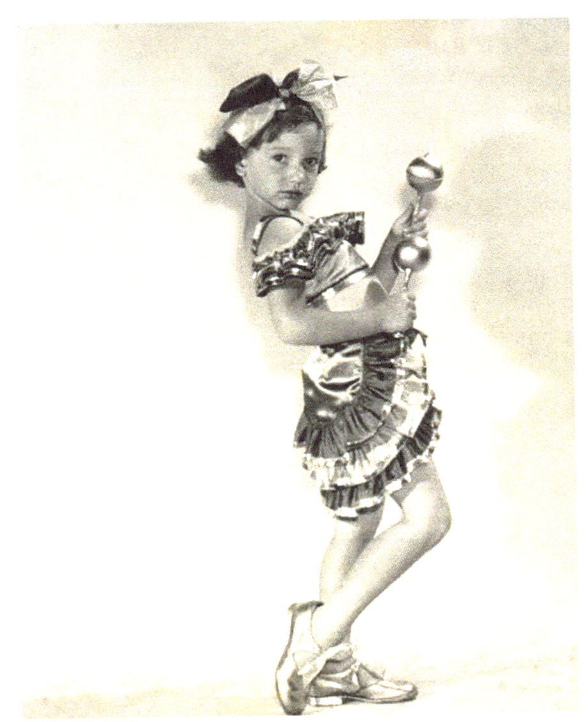

A little tap dancer, merely age five, I was a quite serious, analytical child.

A visual sponge, I was about to imagine my newest creation. Not a dancer at all at that moment, but then floating in color and shimmering satin!

My colorful costume nearly consumed me! Our teacher implored us to smile, but with my head in the clouds, I found myself dreaming and started painting at four.

1958, Age five, Coral Gables, FL

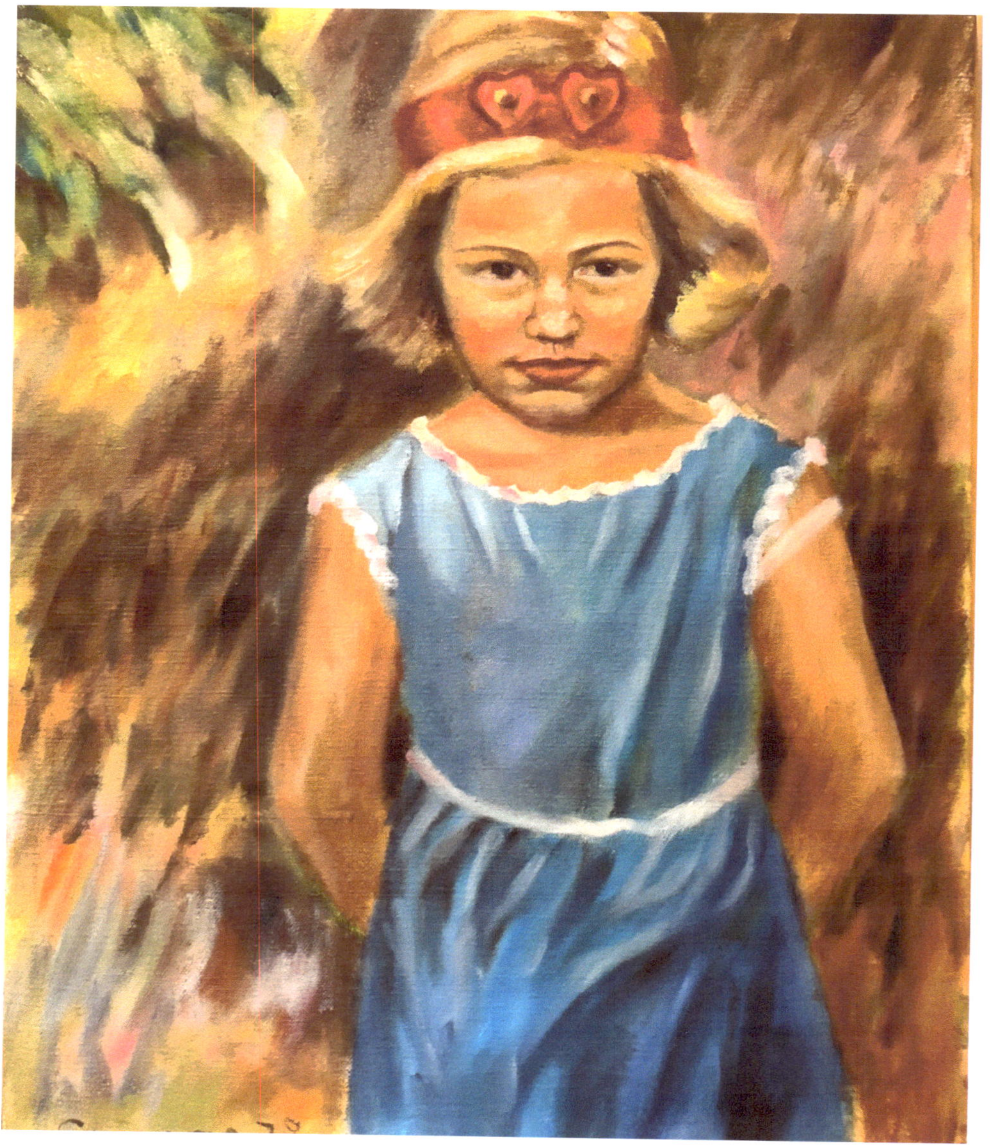

My Little Selfie, circa 1970s
Oil on canvas, 16" x 20"

My
Looking Glass

Looking through, not at the world

With a contemplative stare
Remembering the past and future
The window's always there

Not really mad nor pouting
Just drifting along in youth,
Studying to figure out
What's there and what is truth

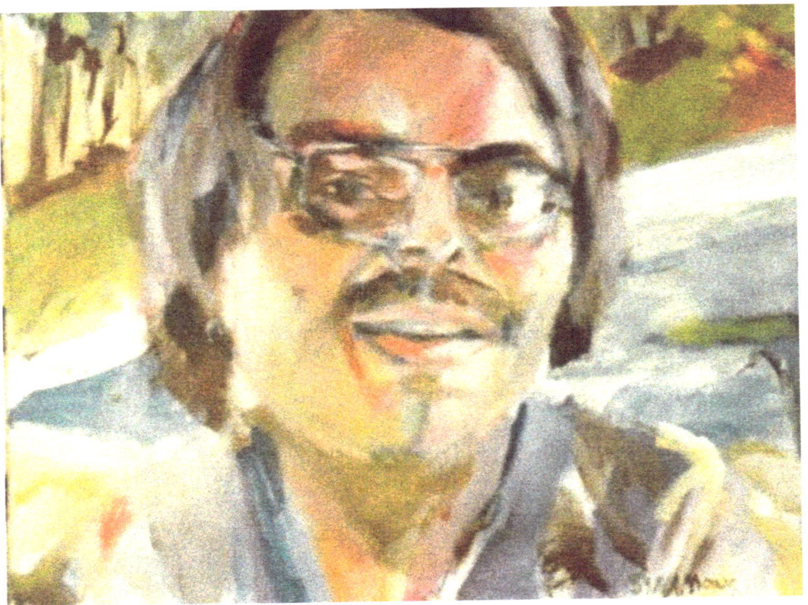

Oh, Miami!

Fleeting, exquisite, minute to minute

The sky paints a picture in unharnessed glory

My eyes are entranced in its hypnotic dance

As each new moment becomes a new story

One of my closest companions in Miami, Jose Martinez-Diaz, lived from 1950 to 2020. A pioneer in his field of clinical psychology, he was the founder of the ABA (Applied Behavioral Analysis) program at FIT (Florida Institute of Technology).

I painted Jose's portrait by the pool while visiting in Miami, FL.

Jose (above), 1978
Acrylic on paper, 11" x 15"

Miami Sky (right), 1978
Oil on canvas, 20" x 20"

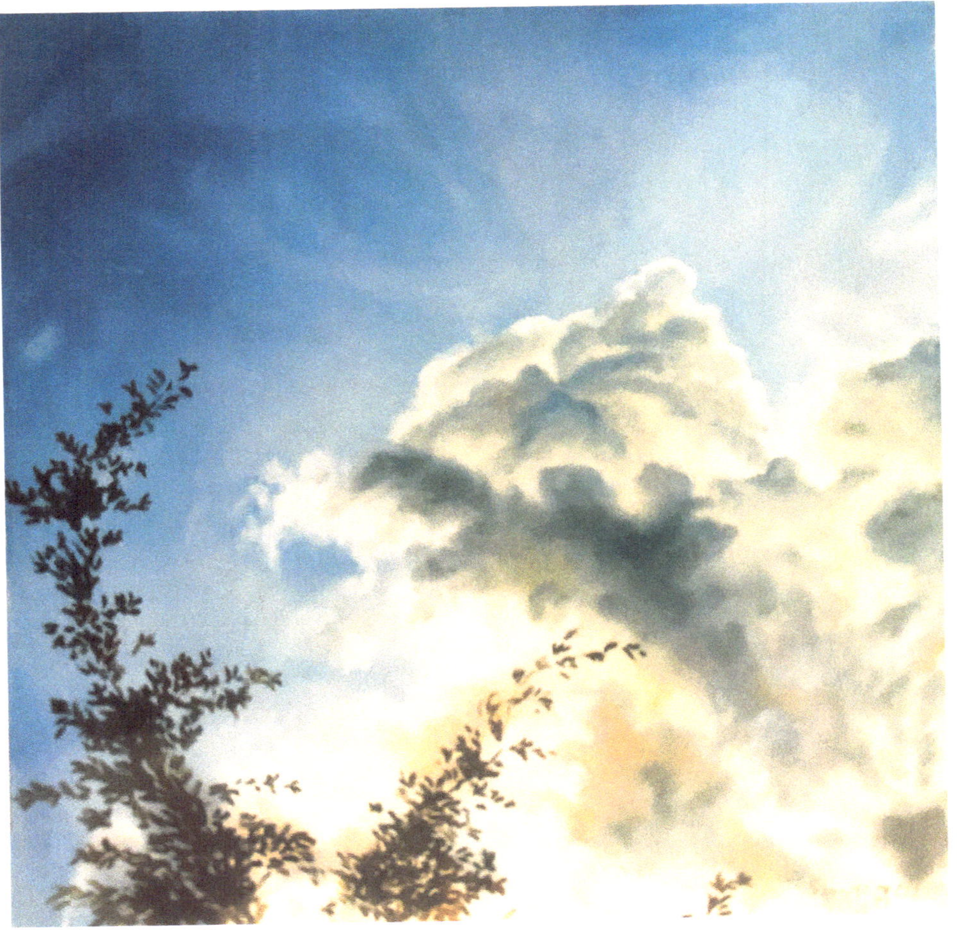

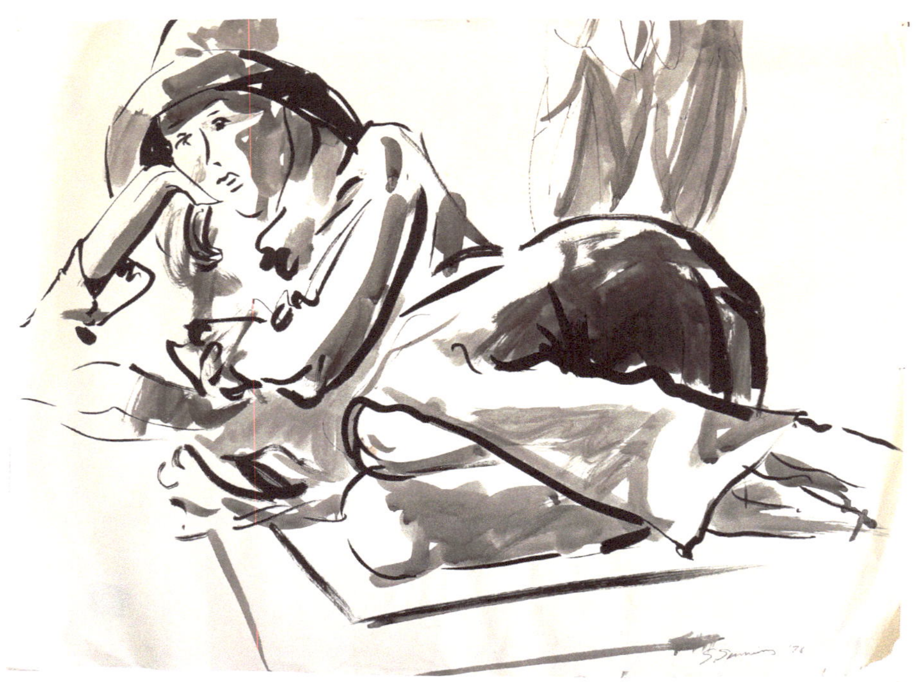

Friends

People come and people go

They're always there

Don't ya know?

Once you've met

They've never left

They're parallel

with your mind and soul

Joyful, grateful, thankful, blessed

Just forget about all the rest

If you don't like it, Throw it away!

Keep joy in heart day to day

Many years have come and gone

May sweet memories always wake you at dawn

School Days (above), 1976
Ink on paper, 16" x 20"

Joy (right), 1978
Watercolor on paper, 11" x 15"

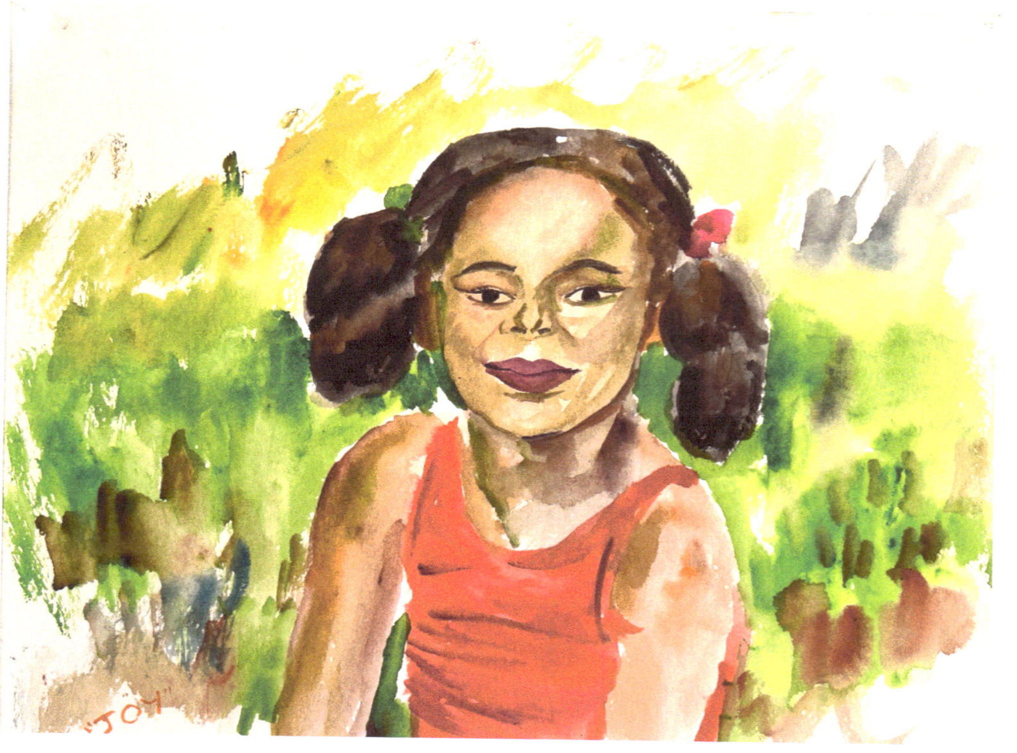

Summer

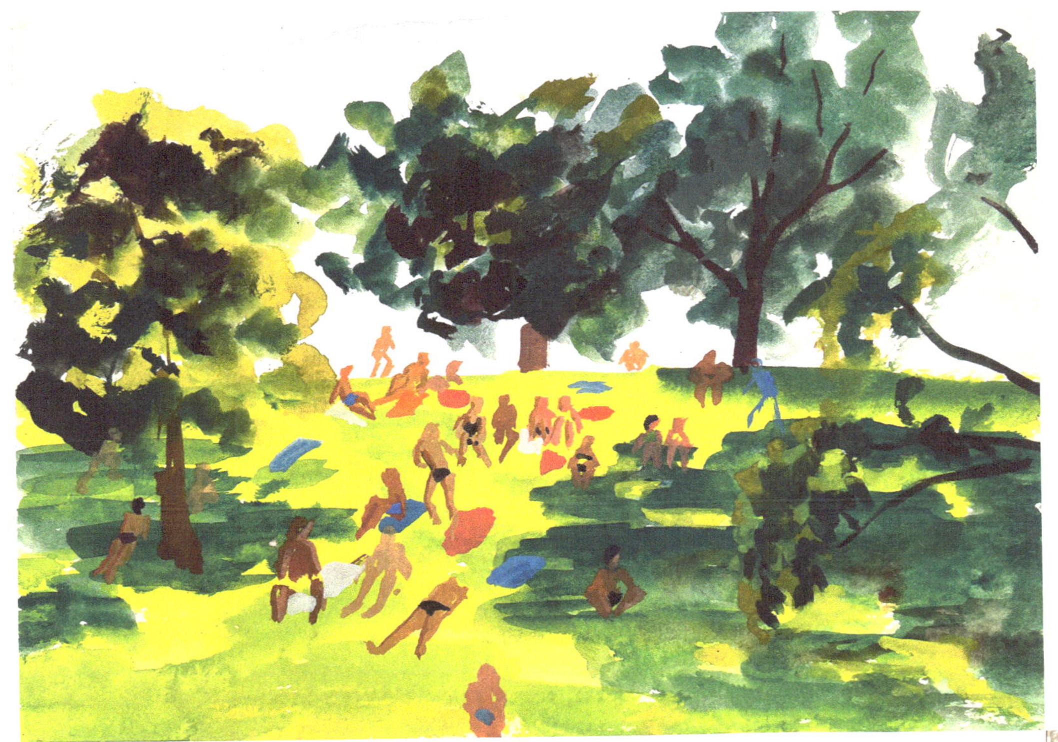

Barton Springs is a happy place
To bask and soak up the sun

Jump in and swim
Cool off your skin
Let's make a plan to do it again!

Drive along a dusty road
And take you where it may
To a swimming place I know and love
This bright and sunny day

Barton Springs (above), 1978
Gouache on paper, 11" x 14"

Goin' Swimming (right), 1978
Watercolor on paper, 8" x 10"

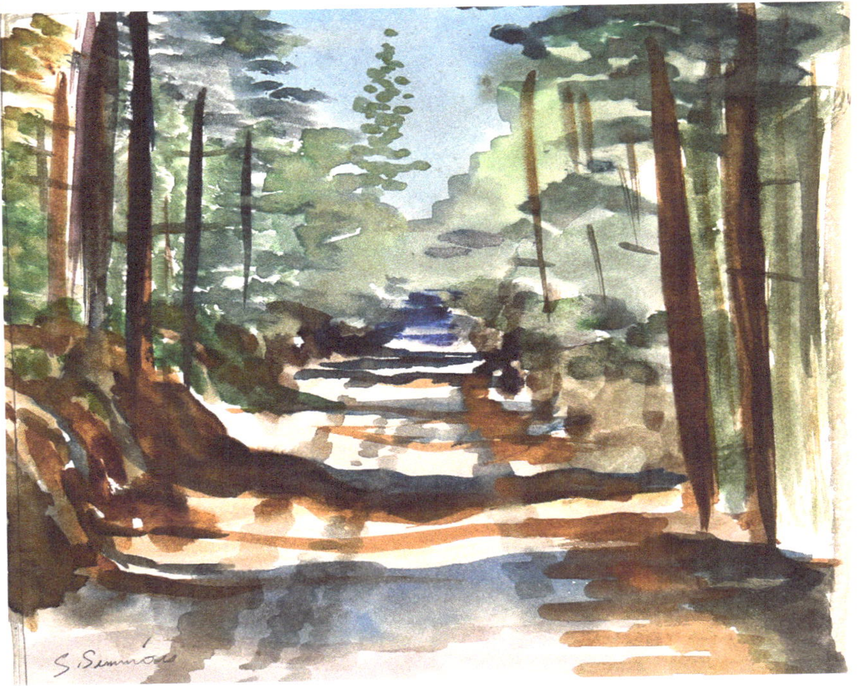

Less is More

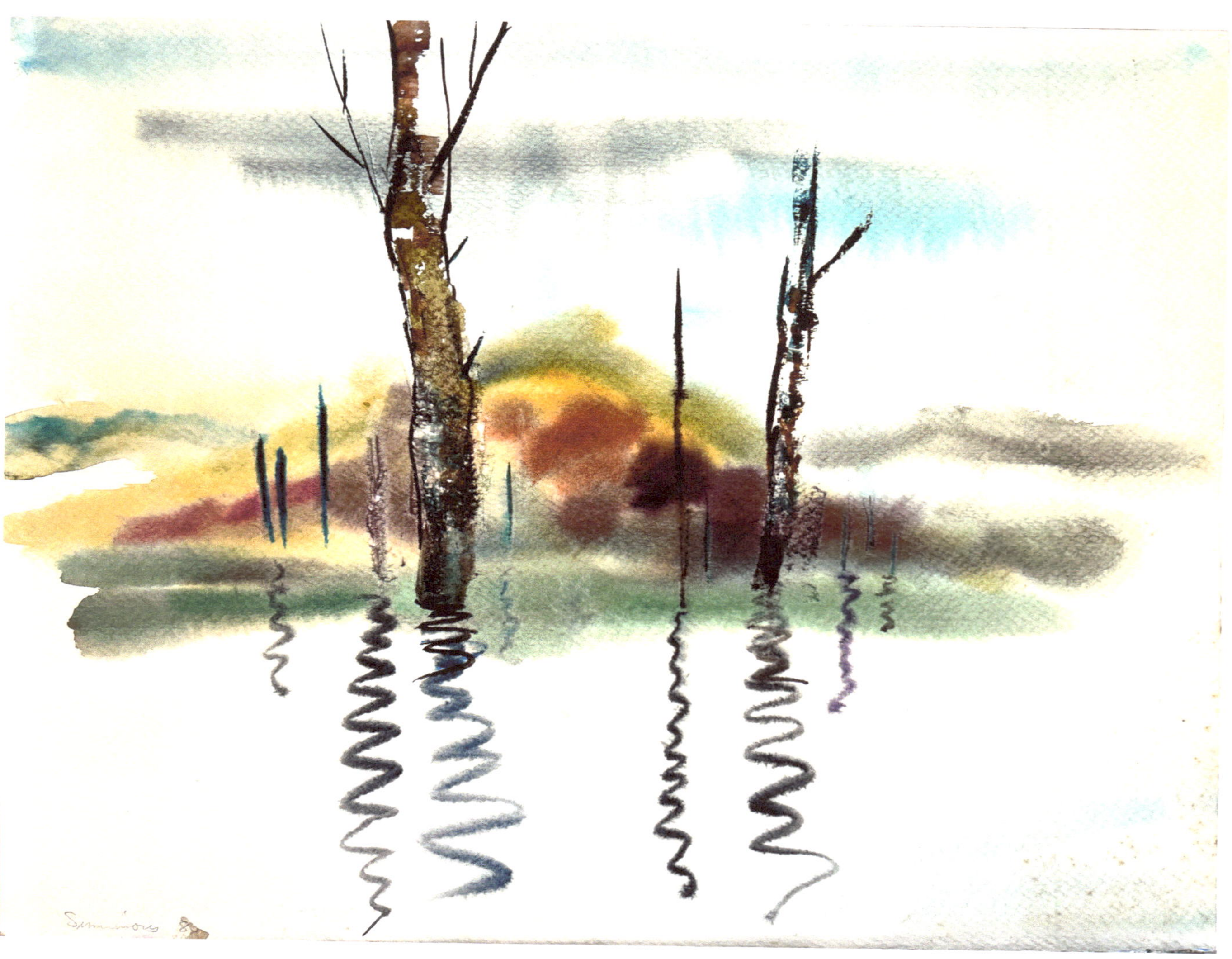

Reflections, 1978
Watercolor on paper, 11" x 15"

My Dog Christel

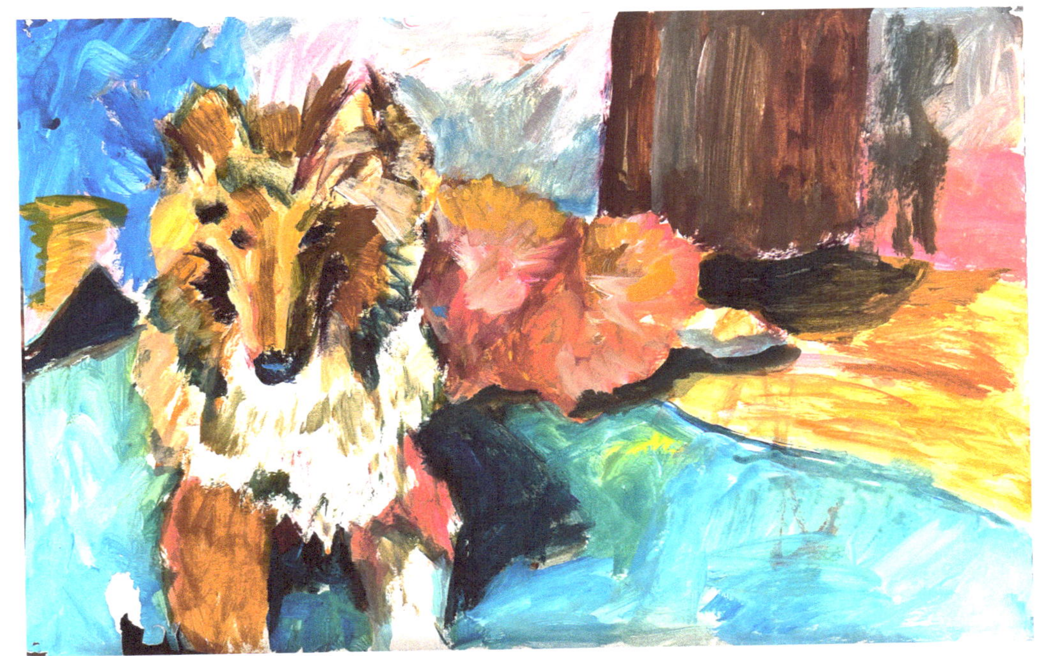

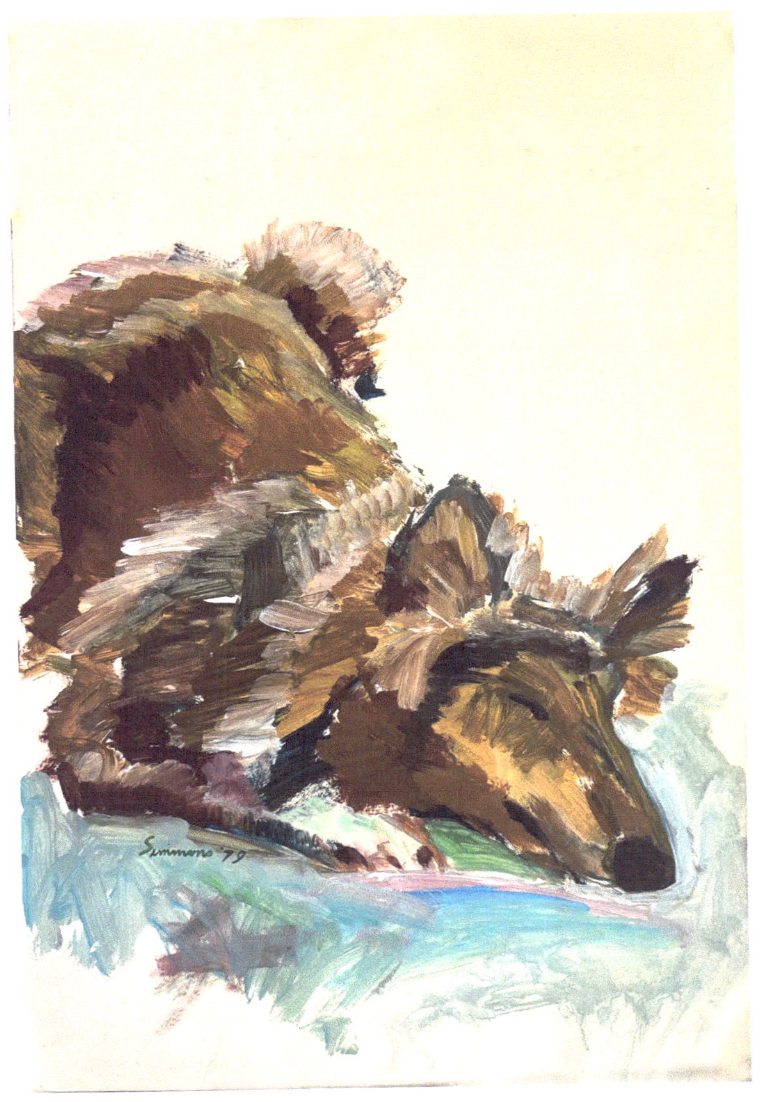

Precious pup, my loyal friend

You kissed my tears goodbye

You'll always be a part of me

You're part of who I am

Christel Sleeping (left), 1979
Acrylic on paper

Playful Christel (above), 1979
Acrylic on paper

Making Friends

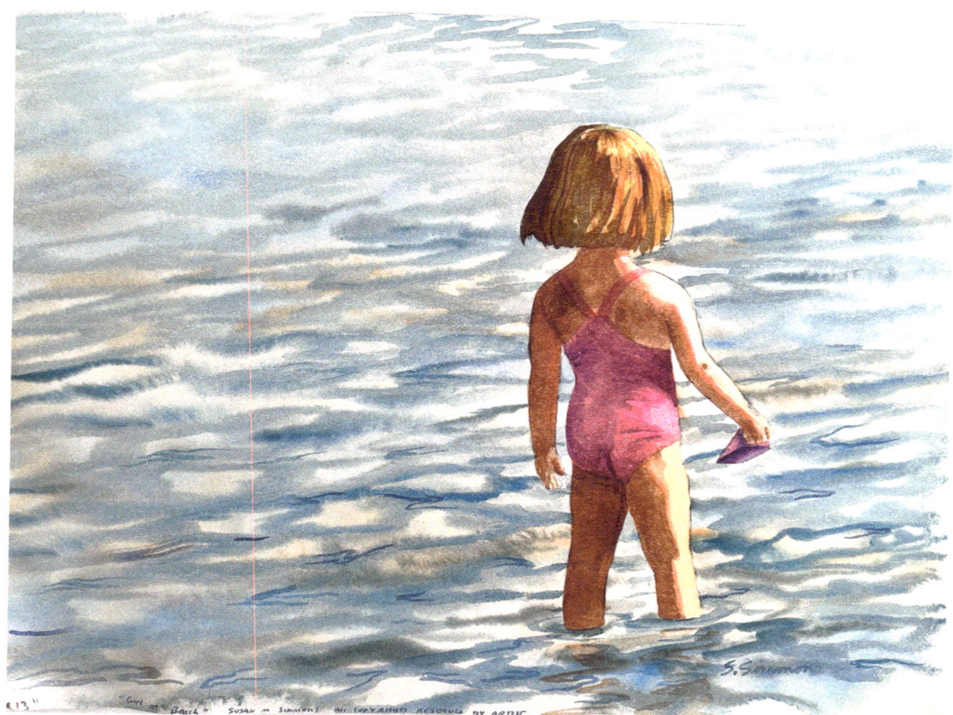

I've got a shovel

What will I find?

I'll give him a gift

If he doesn't mind

Here's my chance to make a new friend

Maybe tomorrow he'll come back again

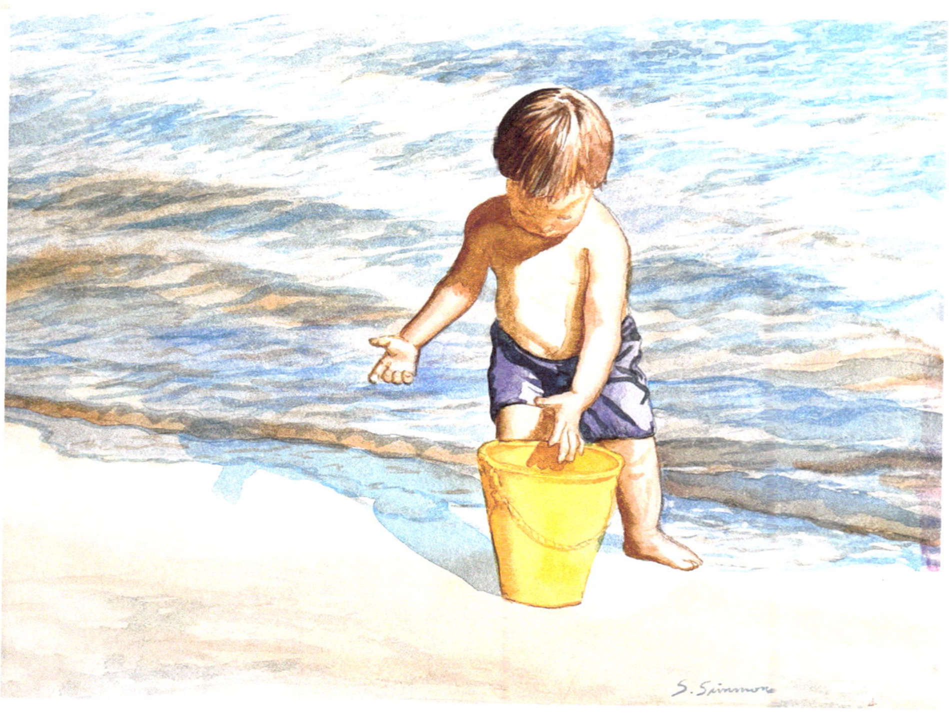

Thoughtful Girl (above), 1979
Watercolor on paper, 11" x 15"

Beach Comber (right), 1979
Watercolor on paper, 11" x 15"

Places

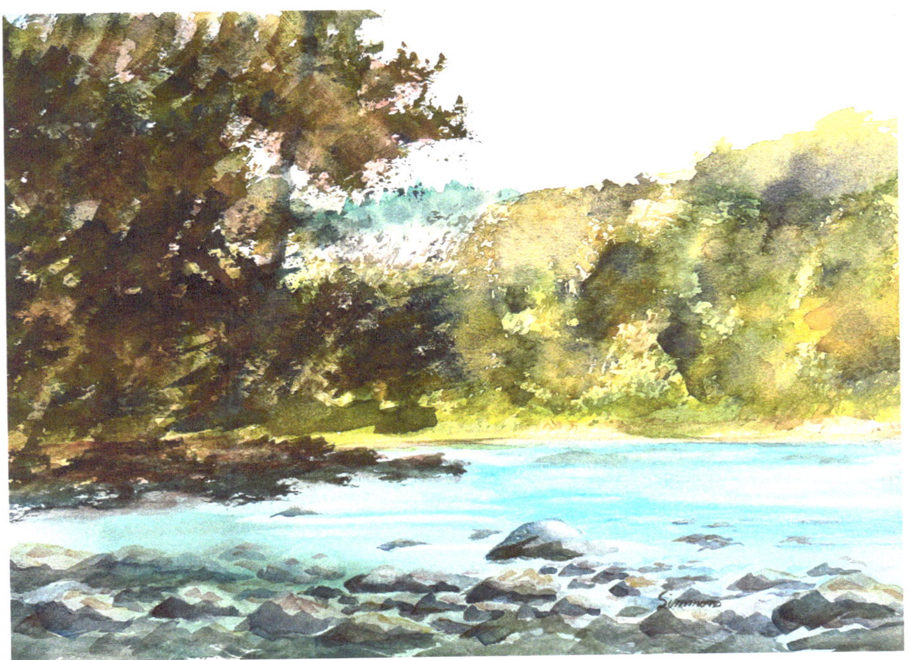

A river speaks volumes

Of time and travel

And carves a path

To ponder and marvel

Speak to me before you vanish

Under the poplar trees

Your songs of glory

Warms my heart

And a promise

Of new beginnings

River Love (above), 1979
Watercolor on paper, 11" x15"

Last Peek (right), 2008
Oil on canvas, 11" x 14"

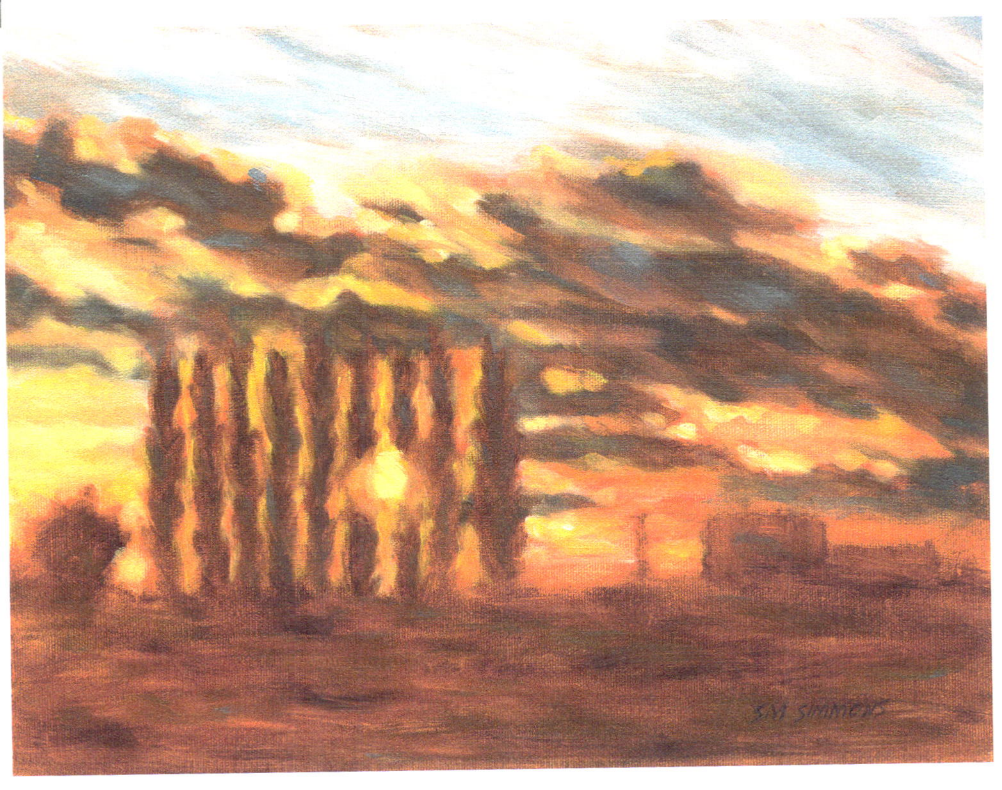

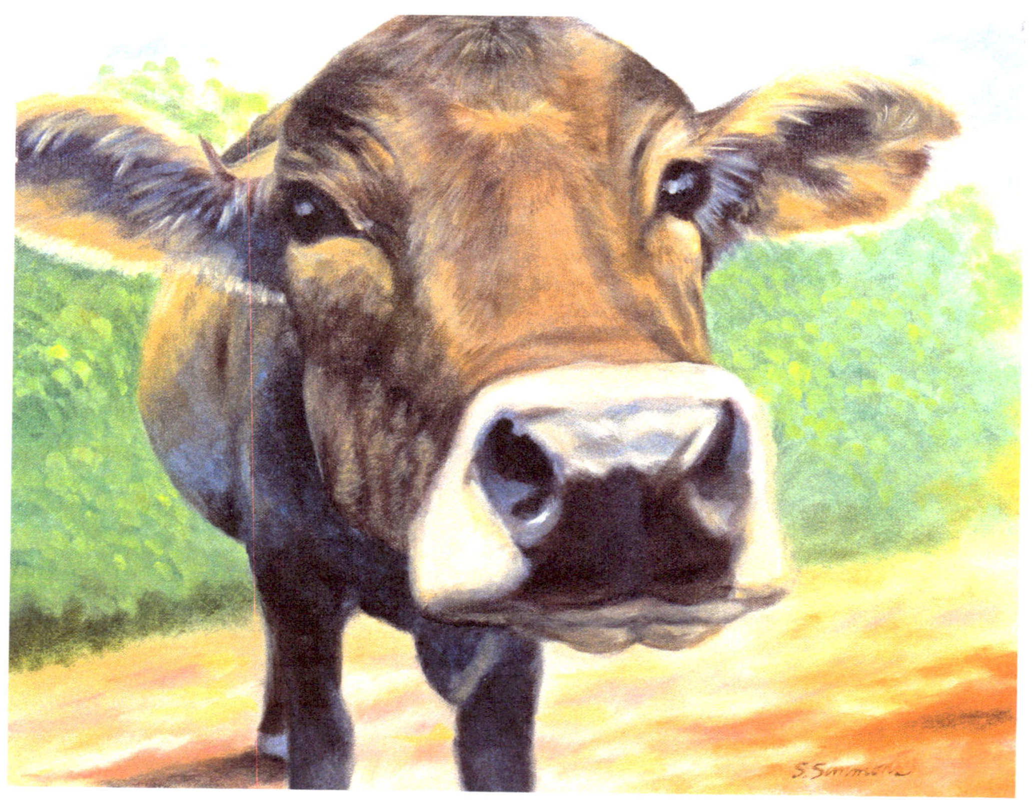

Gratitude

I open my eyes and see all that is there

And disregard all that is not…

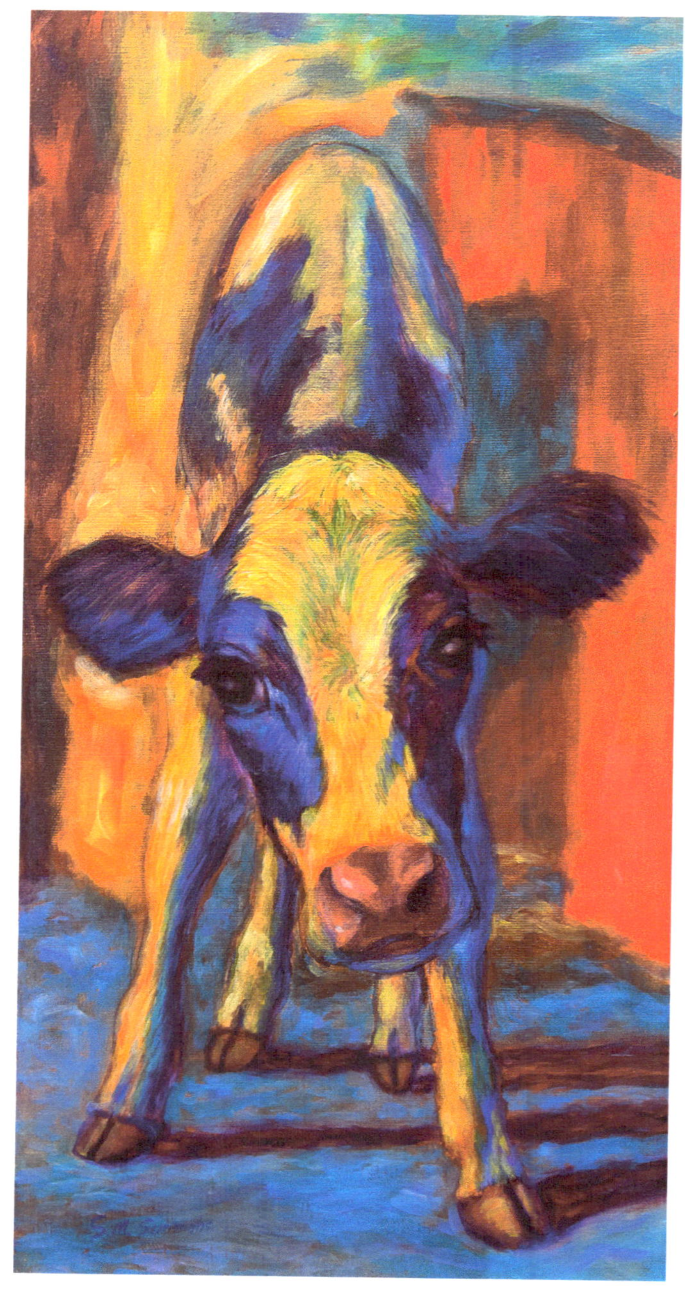

Mona Moo (above), 1991, Oil on canvas, 16" x 20"

Nu Moo in Town, 1998,
Acrylic on canvas, 10" x 20"

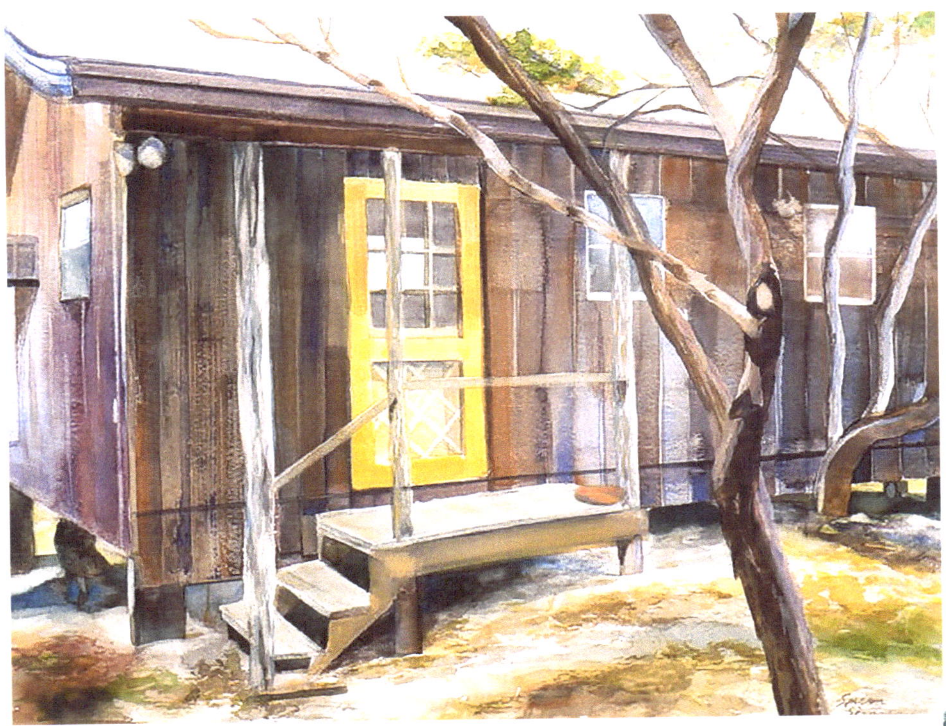

Dad's Cabin

Well-respected, in great demand

My aerospace-Dad engineer

He lived among the clouds at heart

And dreamed of better wings

His brilliance unsurpassed by others

Though he was not boastful at all

He wasn't pompous

But dreaming and planning

And seen by most as awkward

Dad's Cabin (above), circa 1970s
Watercolor, on paper 11" x 14"

Lowell River Walk (right), 2017
Oil on canvas, 11" x 14"

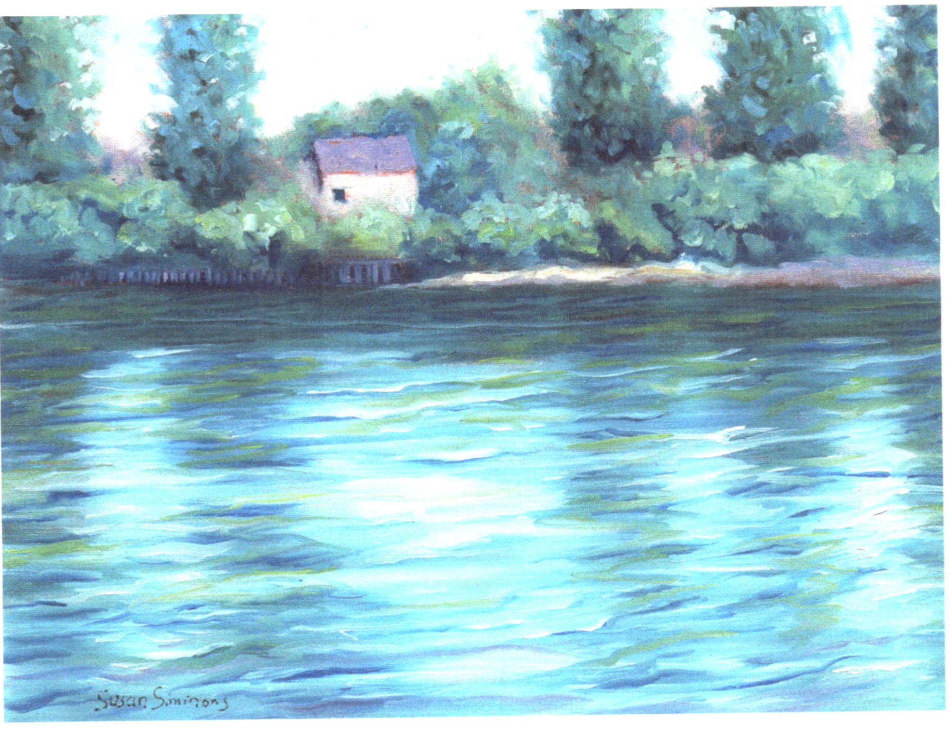

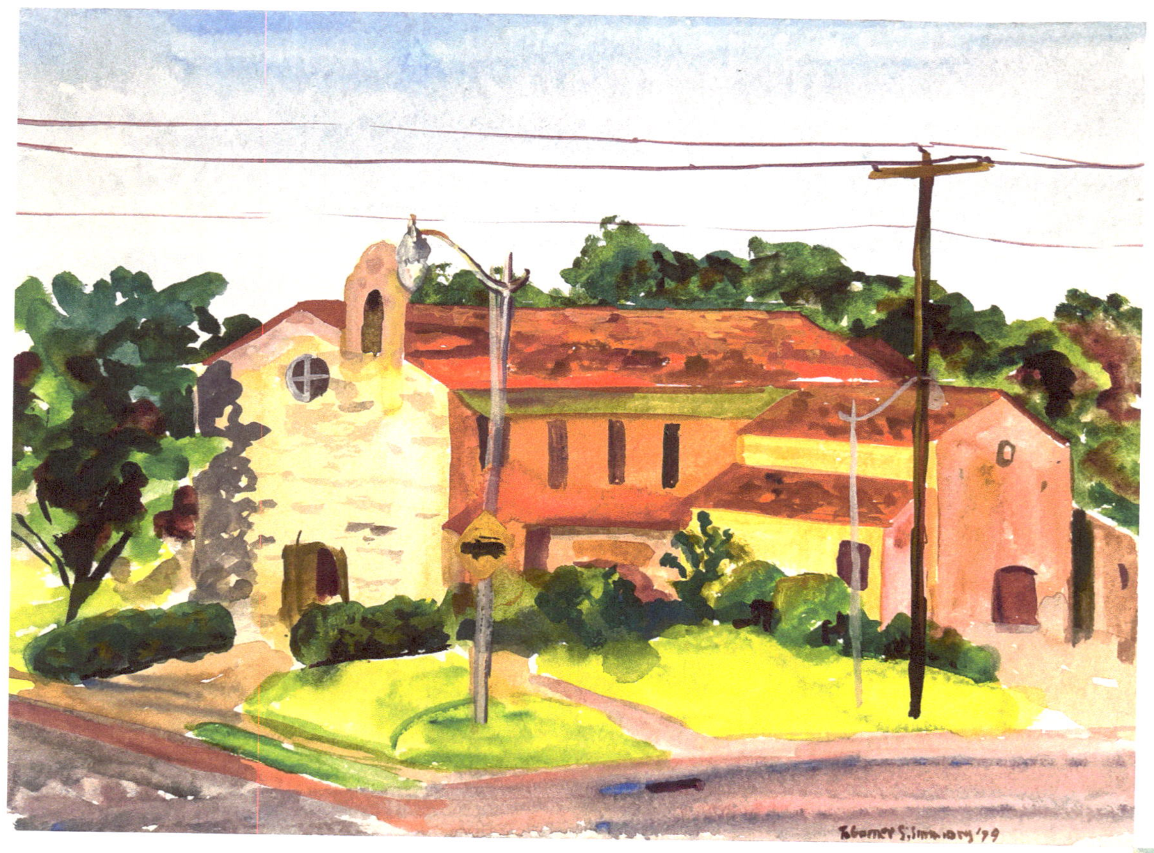

Light

It warms the soul and feeds the trees

Love whispers in the gentle breeze

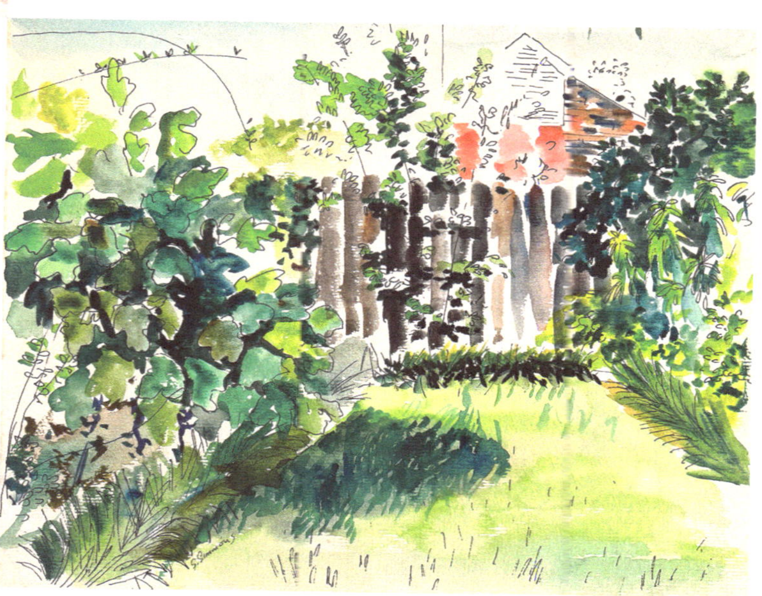

A Place to Gather (above), 1979
Gouache on paper

Summer Garden (right), 1979
Watercolor on paper

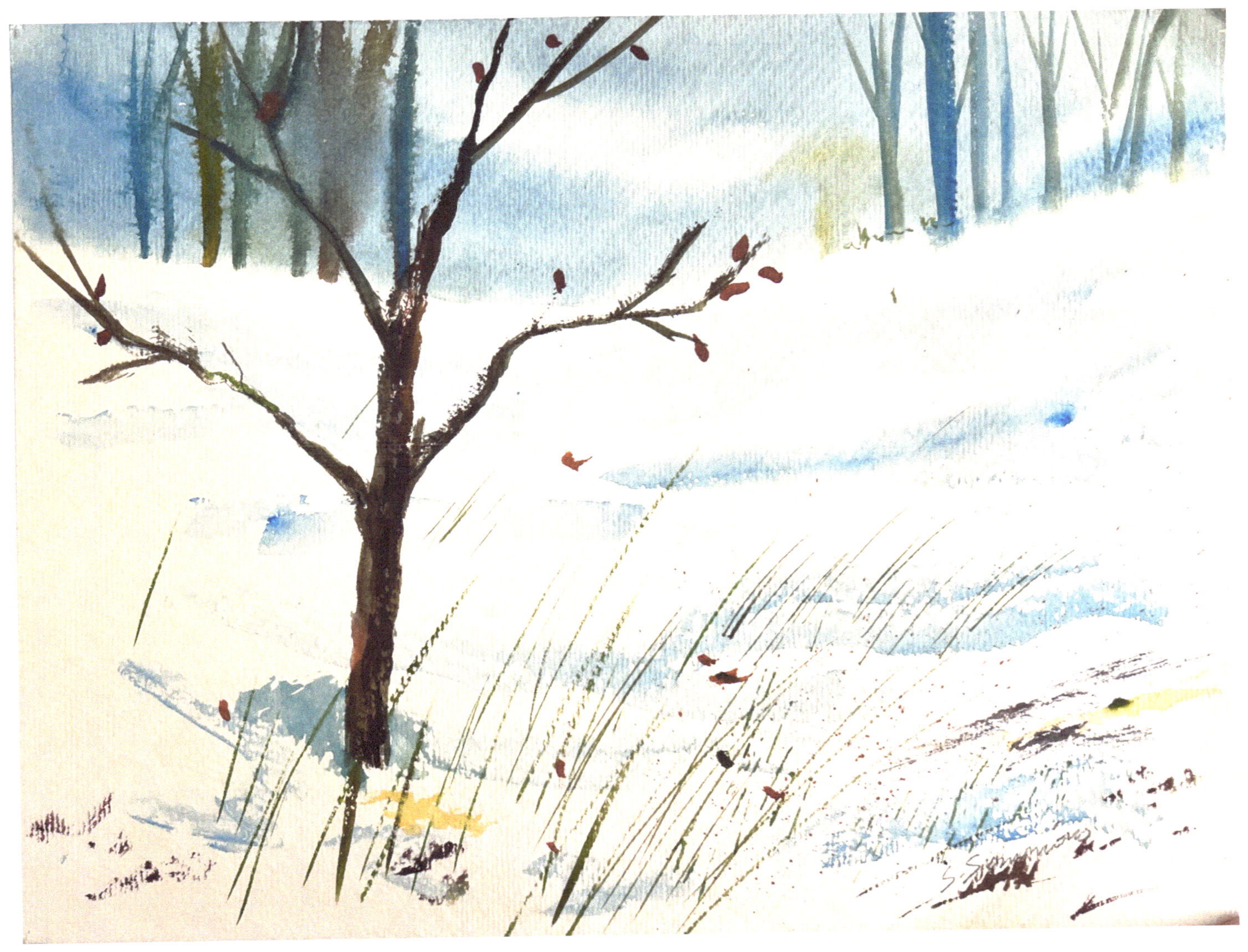

Last of the leaves on a snowy glen

The glory of spring will come again!

Winter, spring, summer, and fall

Favorite season? I love them all!

A Snowy Glen, 1979
Watercolor on paper

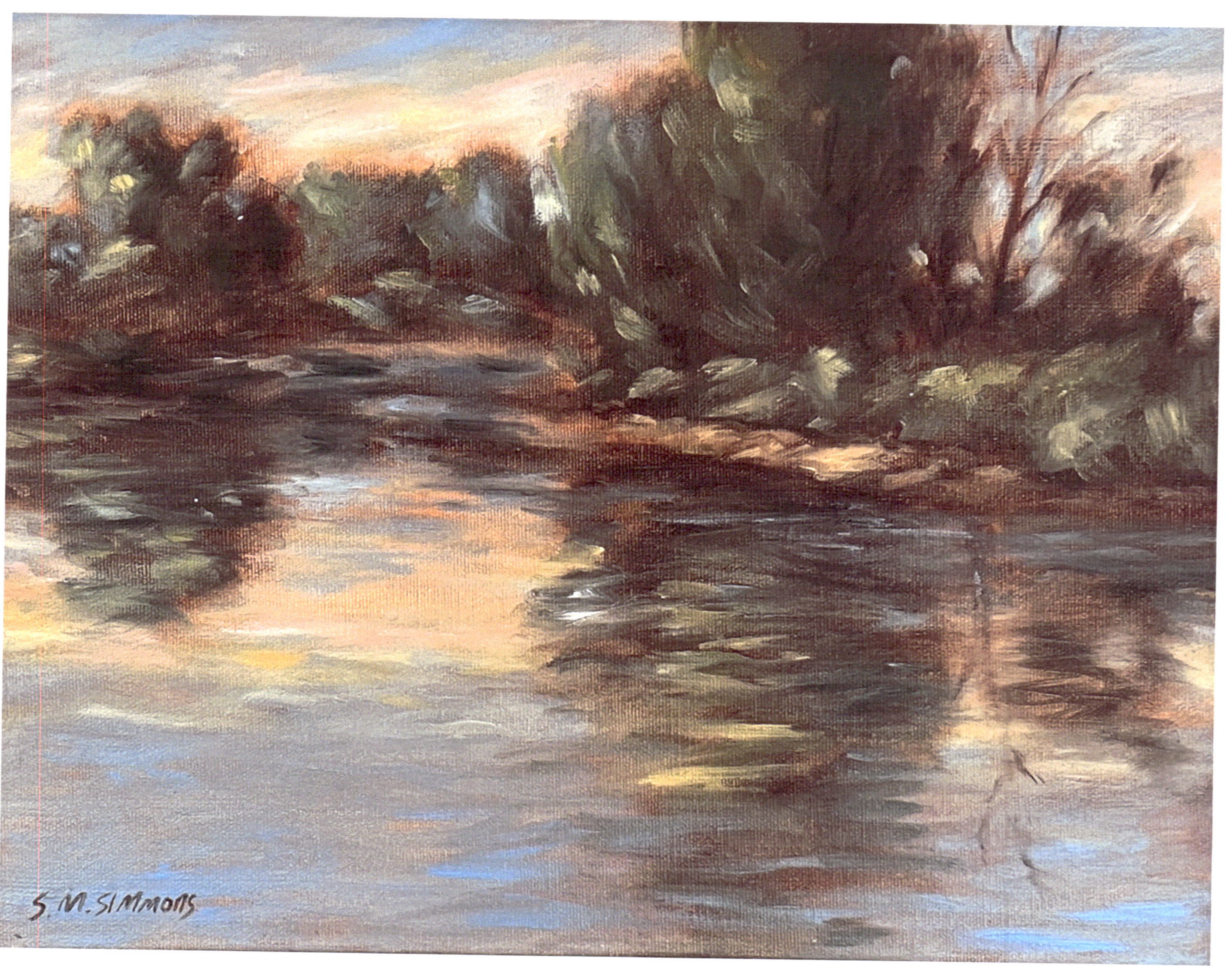

Waterplay, circa 1990s
Oil on canvas, 11" x 14"

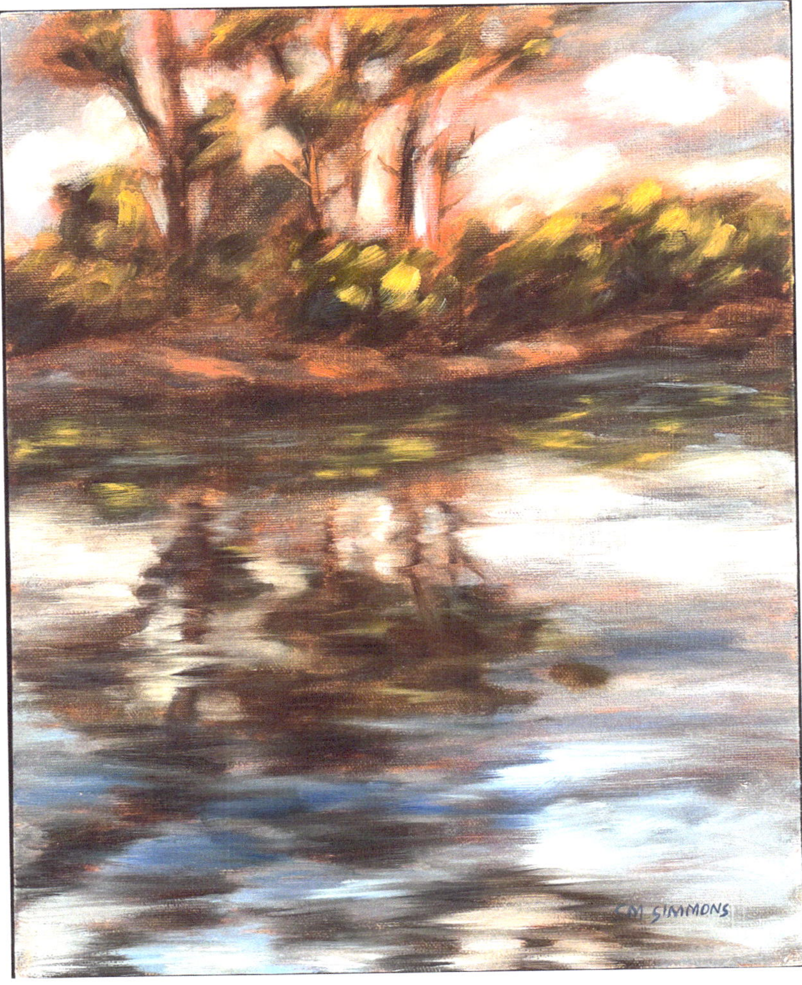

Shades and shadows of gray and rust

Dark and dismal, full of dust

Through my silent unraveling place

I recover beauty in this place

Colorful feasts my brush unfurls

The splendor of warmer days untold

Play, sweet sky on the river-ride

with breath of color that dance my eyes wide!

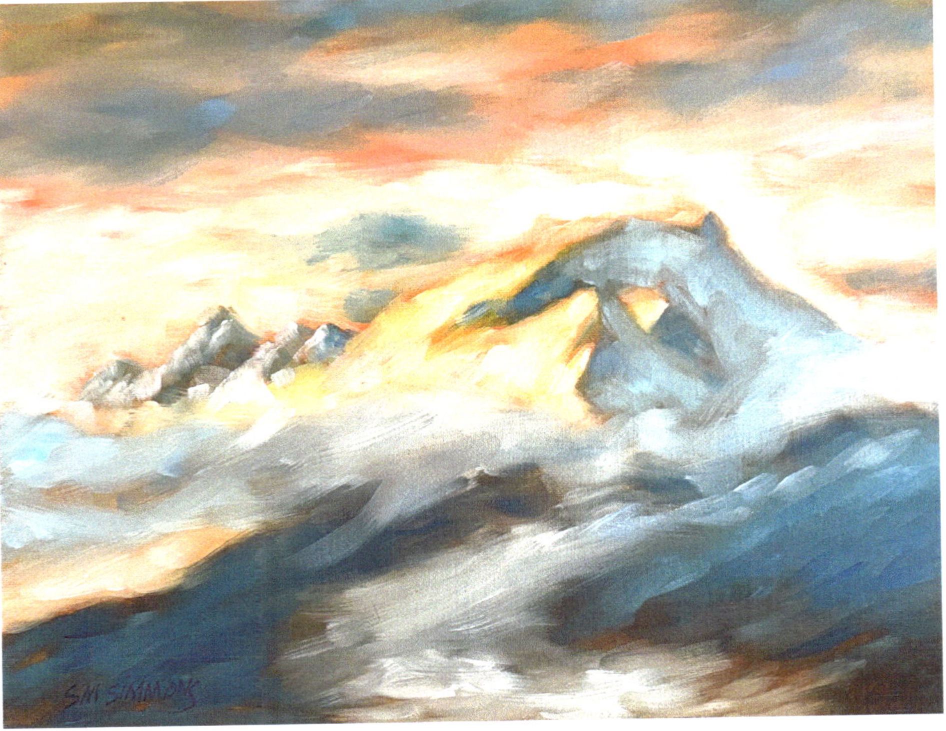

Swift (above), circa 1990s
Oil on canvas, 11" x 14"

Rainier Glow (right), circa 1990s
Oil on panel, 11" x 14"

Whisked away beyond this world
Where did you go?
I miss you so

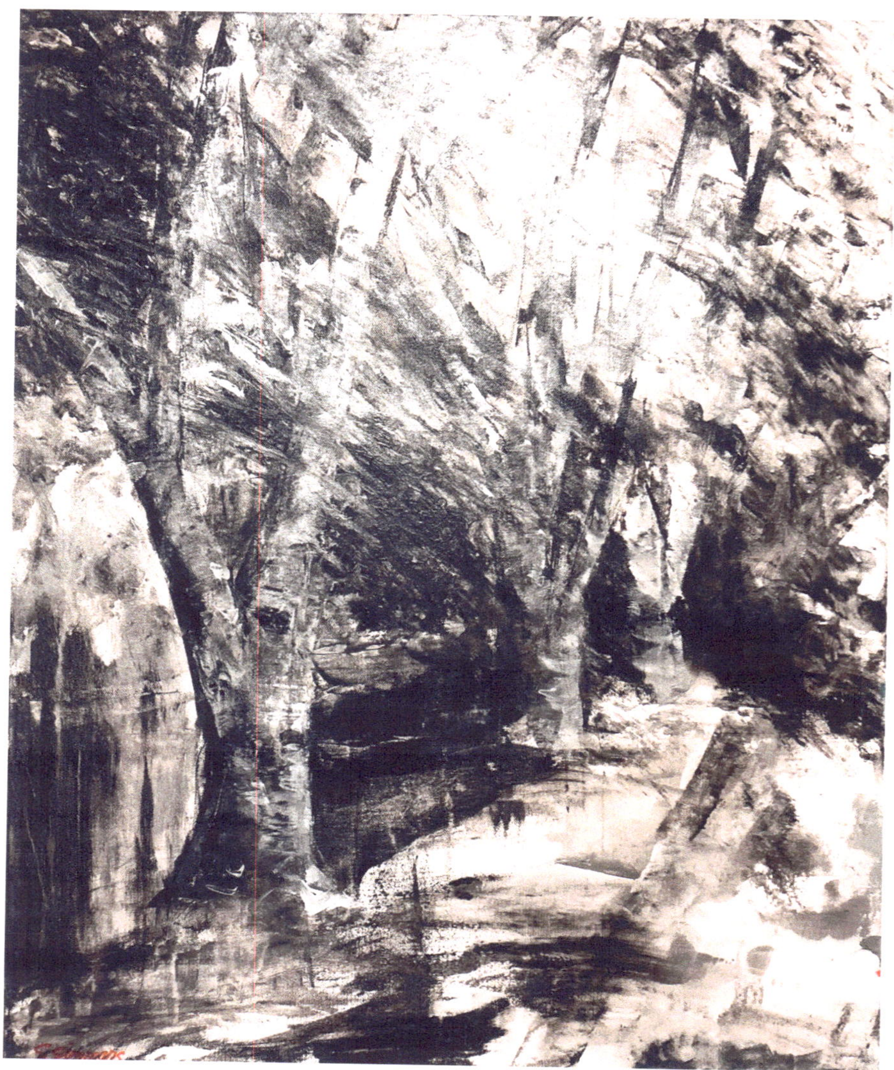

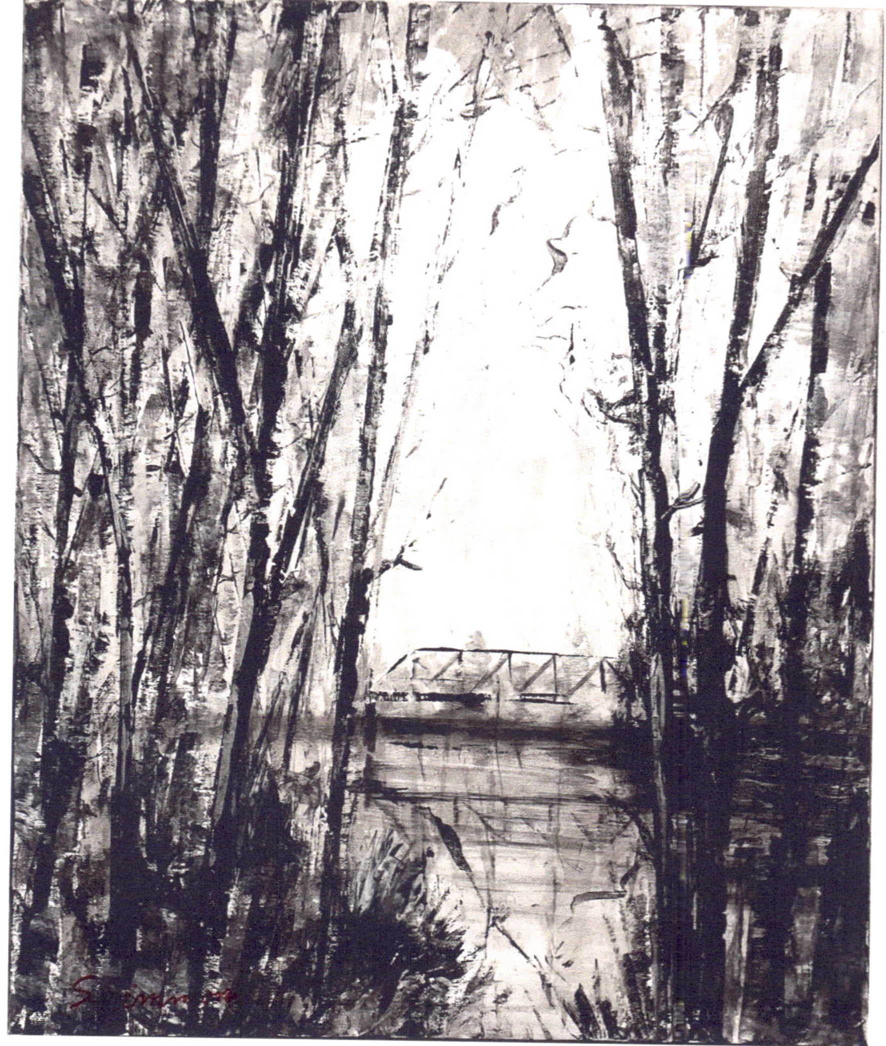

GREY MATTERS

Jason's Place (left), 2018
Acrylic on canvas, 18" x 24"

Breathe (above), 2018
Acrylic on canvas, 16" x20"

The Light?

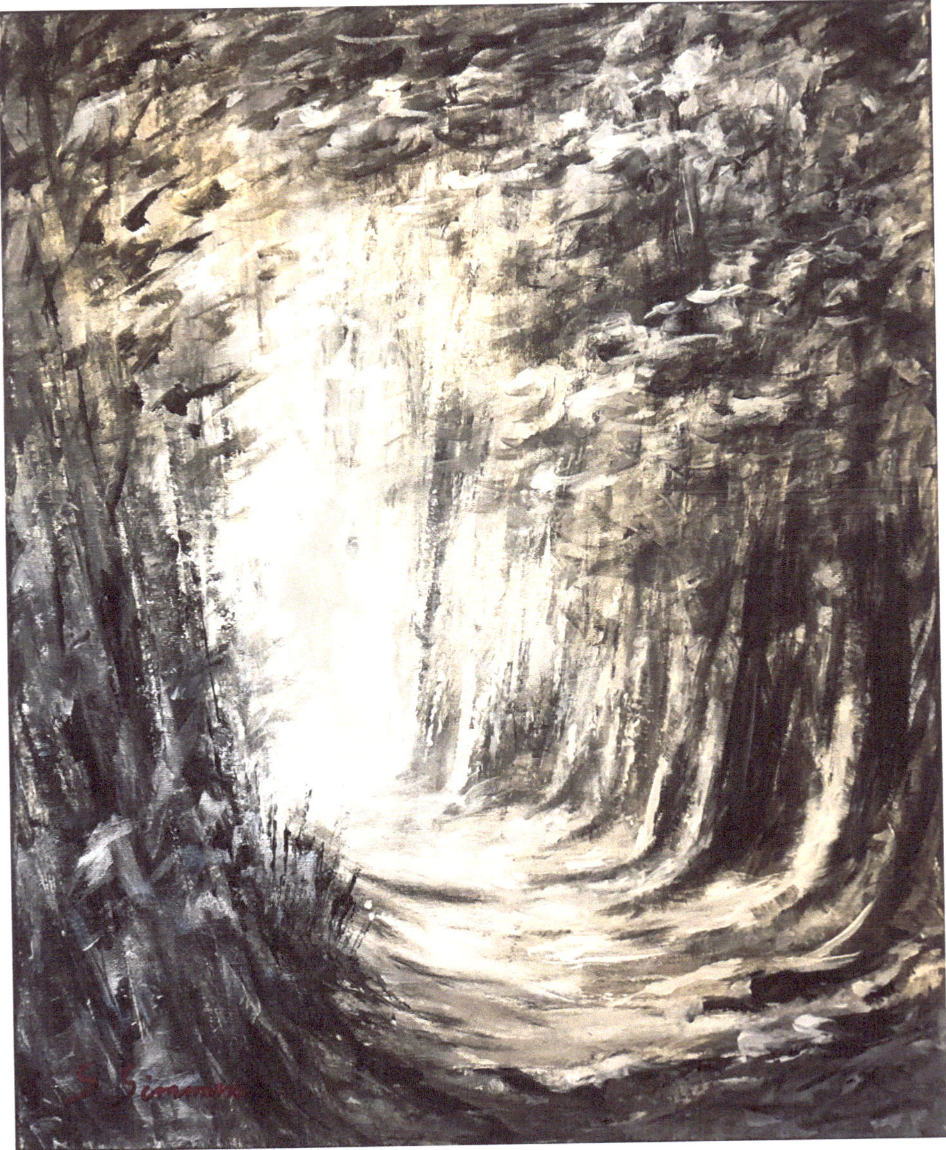

Into the Light (above), 2018
Acrylic on canvas, 16" x 20"

Peace Quest (right), 2018
Acrylic on canvas. 10" x 10"

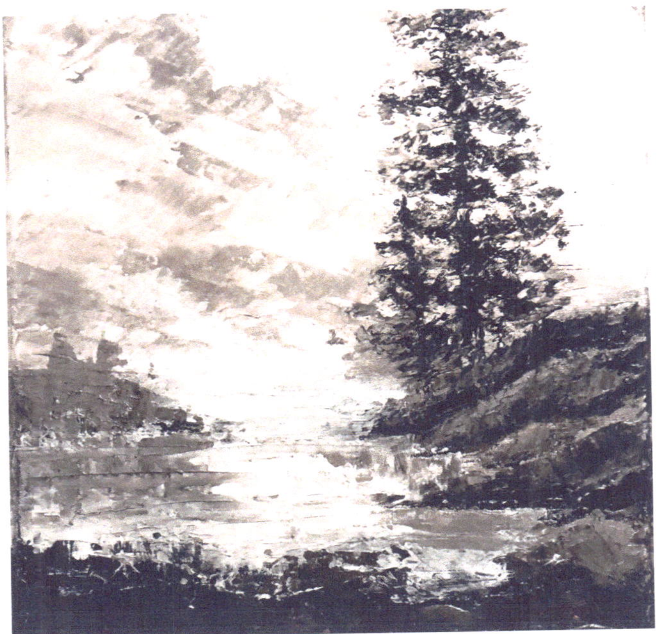

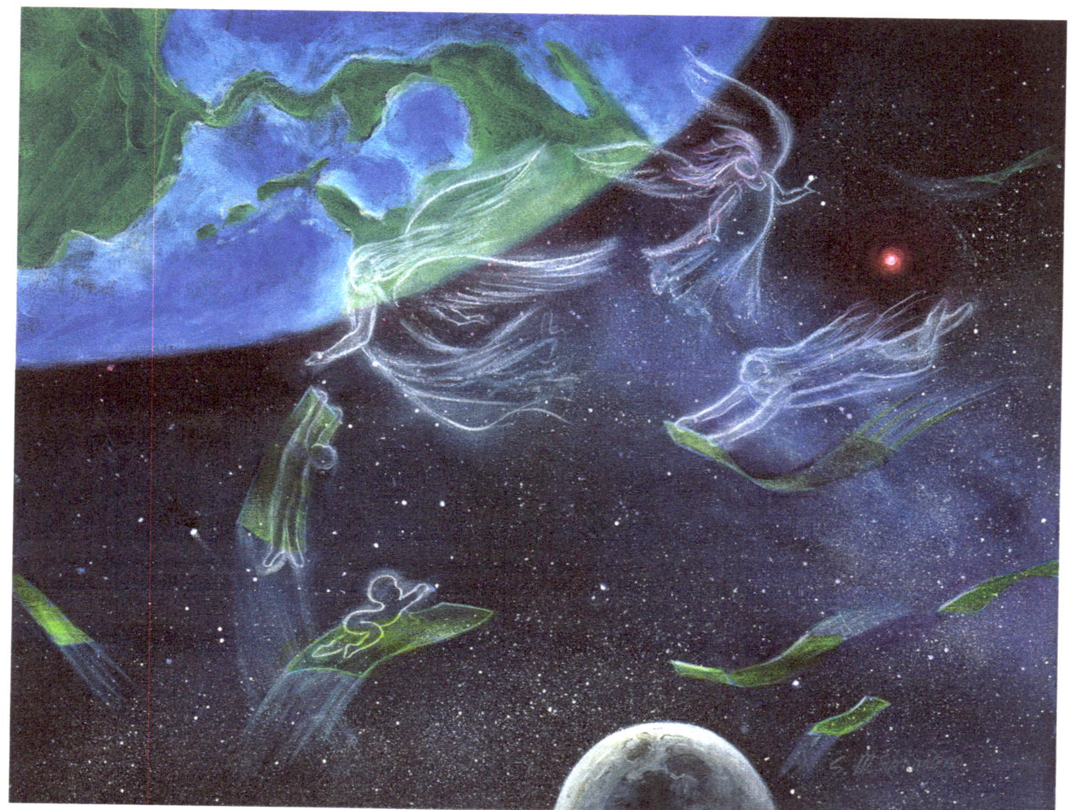

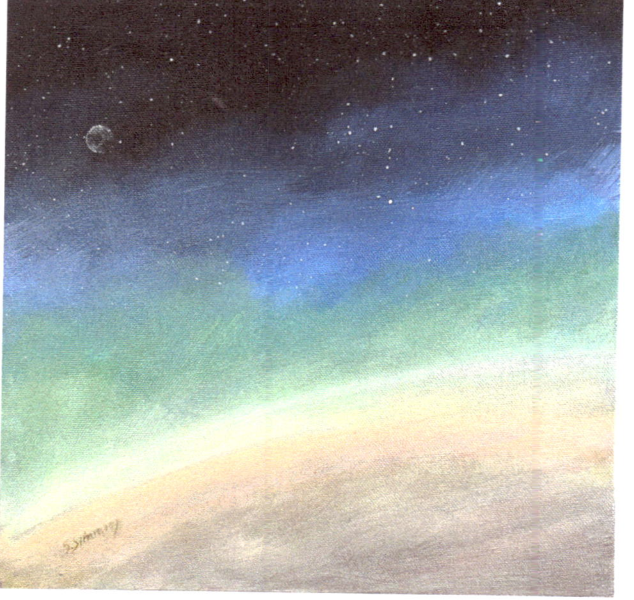

A mystery, this life on earth

Perhaps beyond all reason

By luck, by draw

or through intent

For a lifetime or a season

I am grateful

Green Cards (above), 2020
Acrylic on canvas, 16" x 20"

Traveling Light (right), 2022
Acrylic on canvas, 14" x 14"

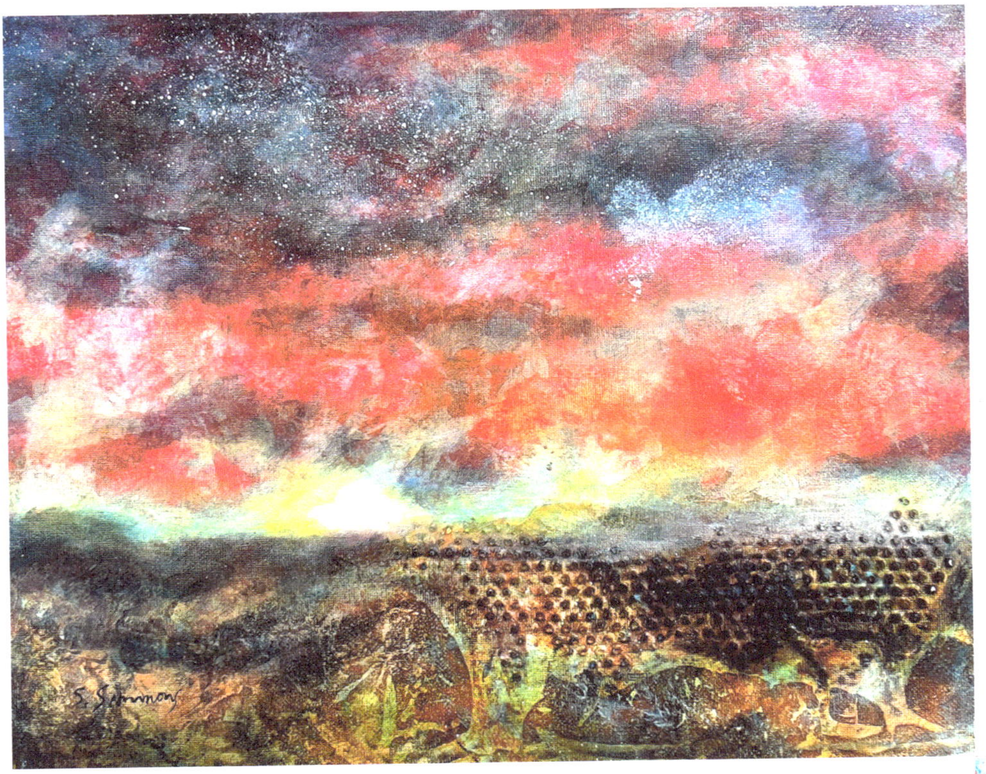

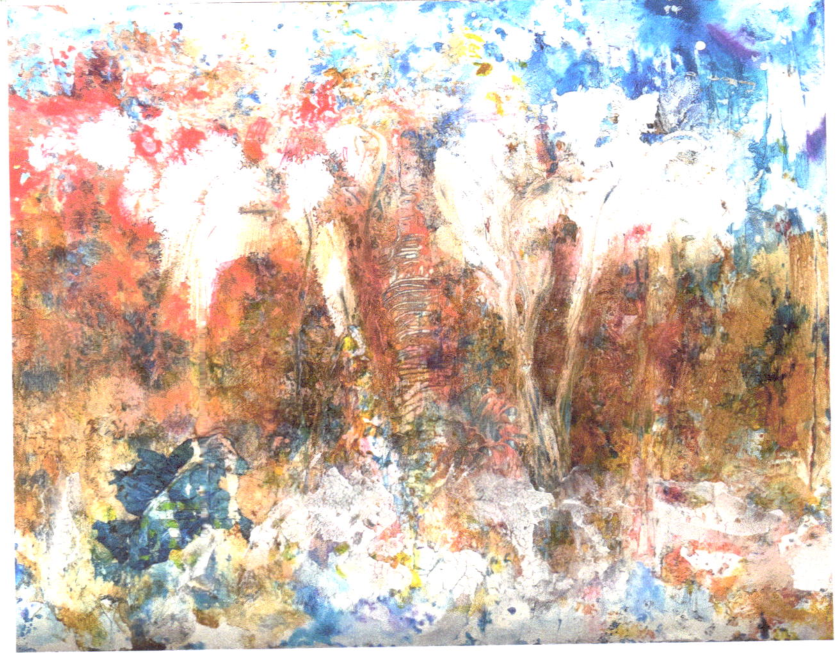

The Red Shift (above), 2020
Acrylic on canvas, 11" x 14"

Uptake (right), 2020
Acrylic on board, 8" x 10"

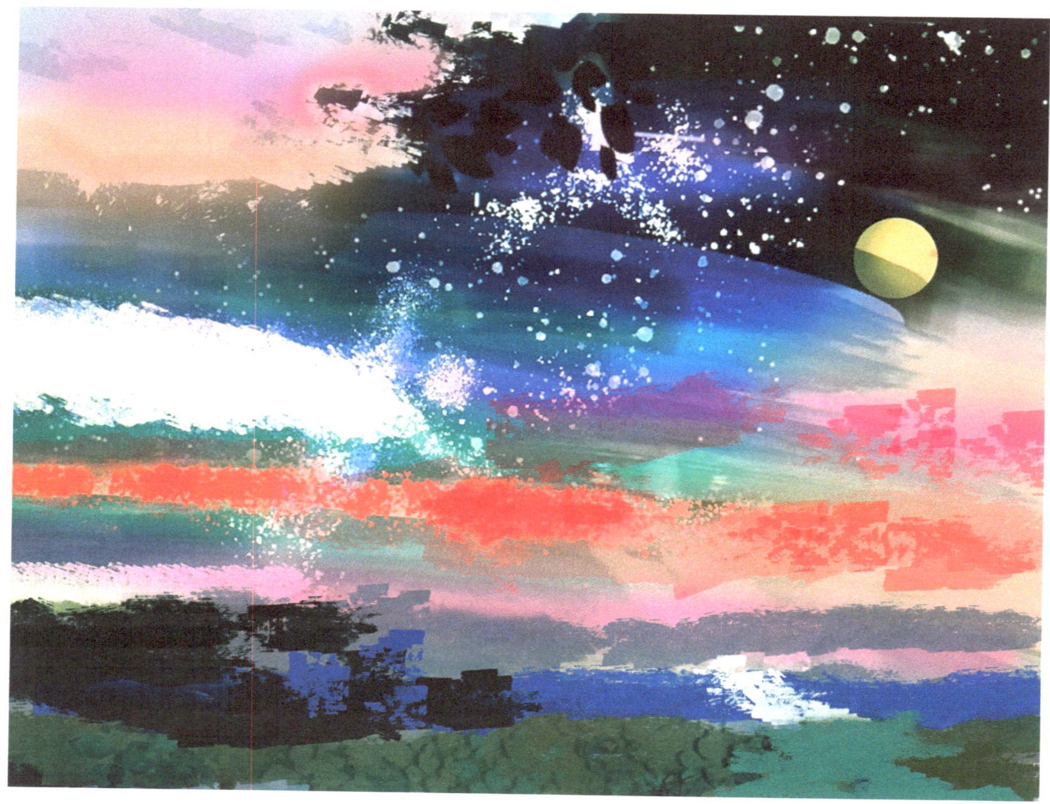

Leaves grow, snow blows

Gone are days of seasons past

Though some remain,

patterns twist

A blip in the radar

takes its turn

Unexpected, unforeseen

I stop to process how I feel

Looking for something a bit more real

I open myself up to the light

Expression comes in many forms

And takes its turn to make it known

Beyond the veil it comes to me

What's there beyond I may have missed

Wings of Light

Angel (above), 2020
Acrylic on board, 11" x 14"

Celestial Guide (right), 2021
Mixed media, 11" x 14"

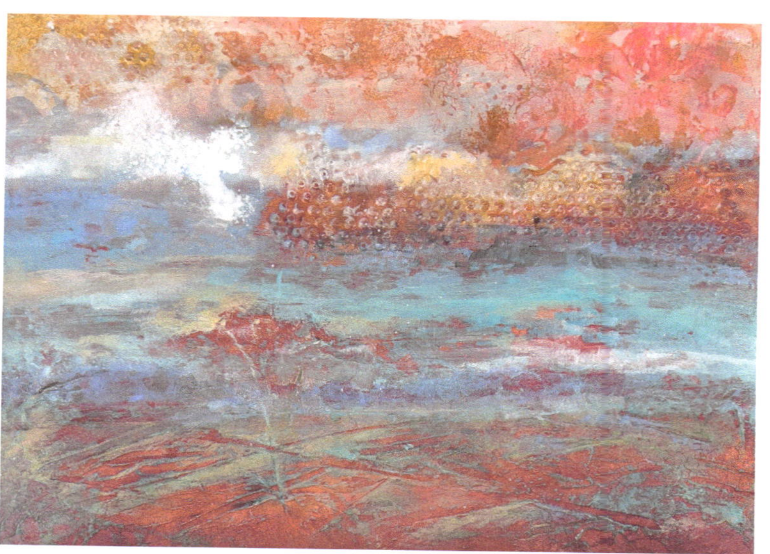

Grounding

With a scrambled heart

I pray for peace

Deep within my soul

The Creator knows

And guides my hands

Color plays its role

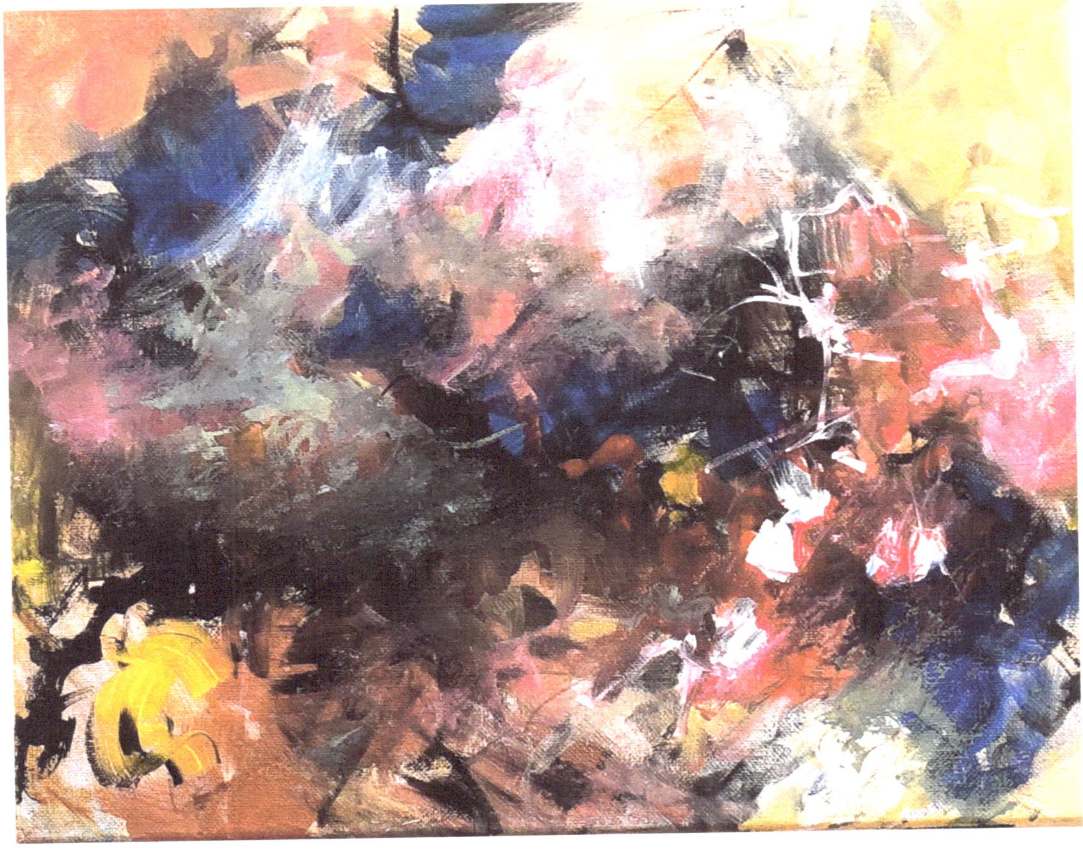

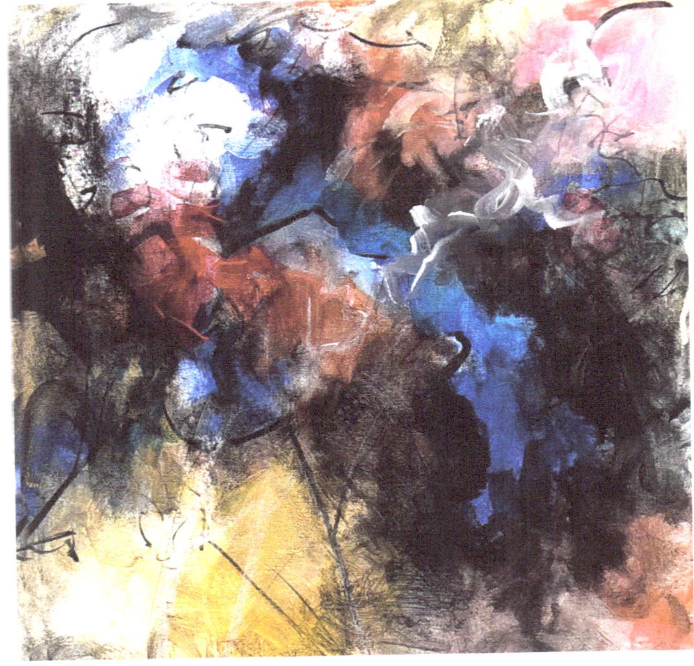

Scrambled Pair, 2021
Acrylic on canvas
Top: 11" x 14", right: 14" x 14

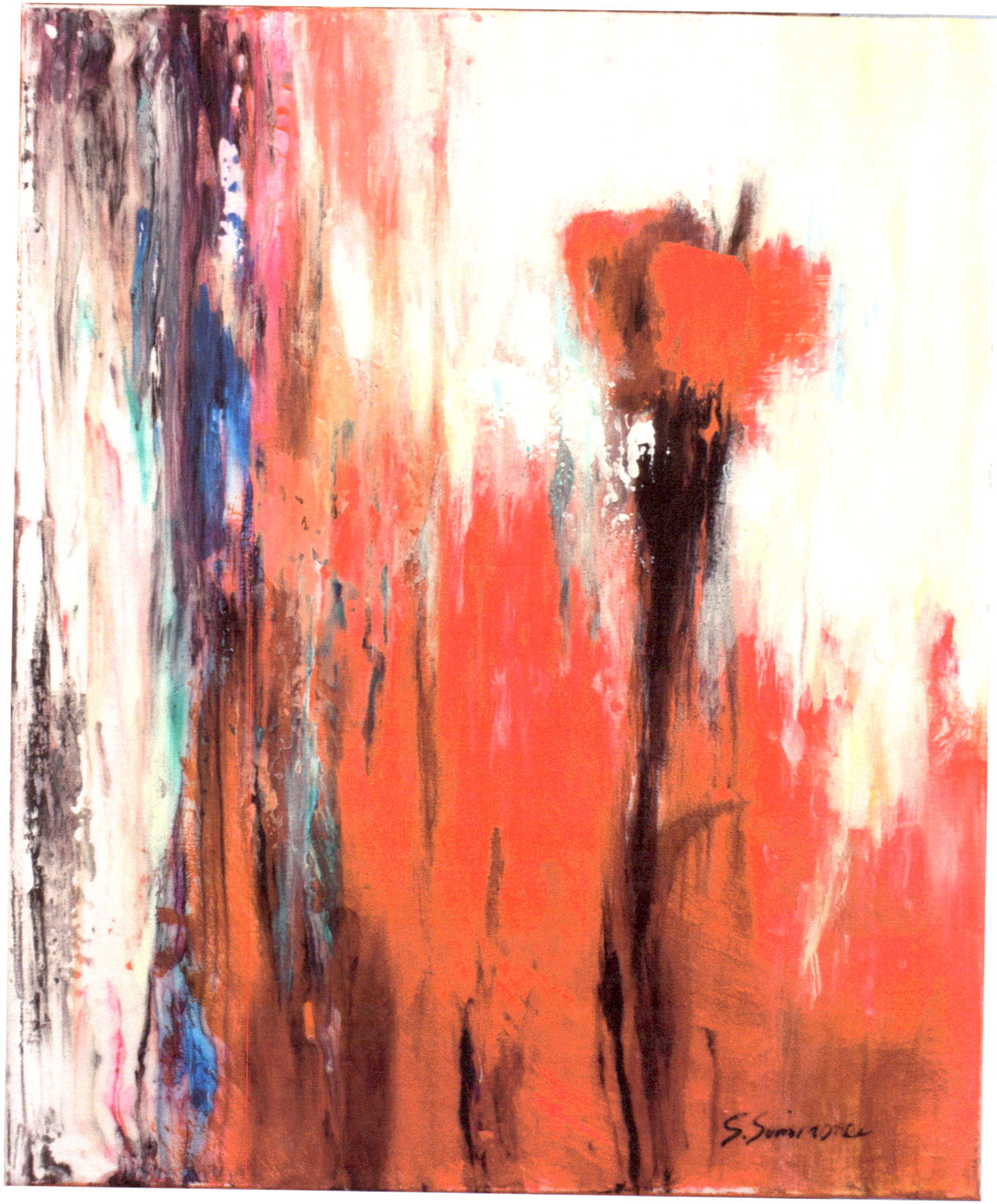

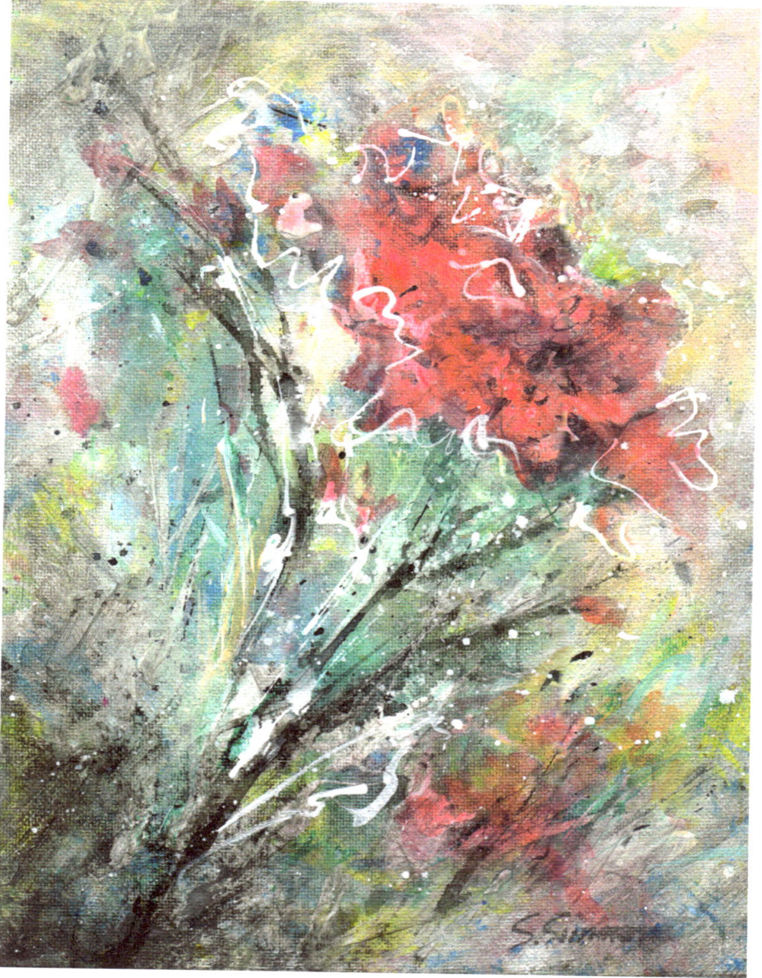

A Flower in Rain (above), 2021, Acrylic on canvas, 16" x 20"
Sweet Allure, (right) 2021Acrylic on canvas, 8" x 10"

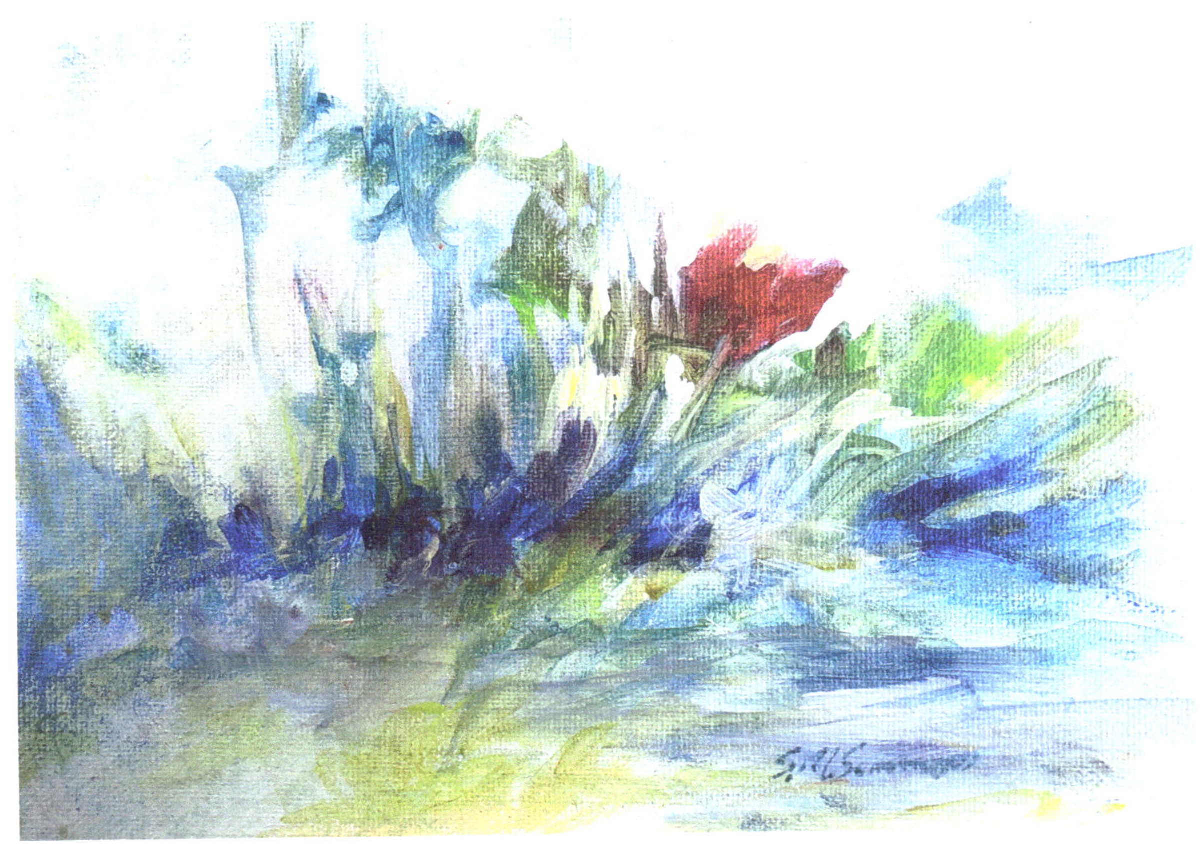

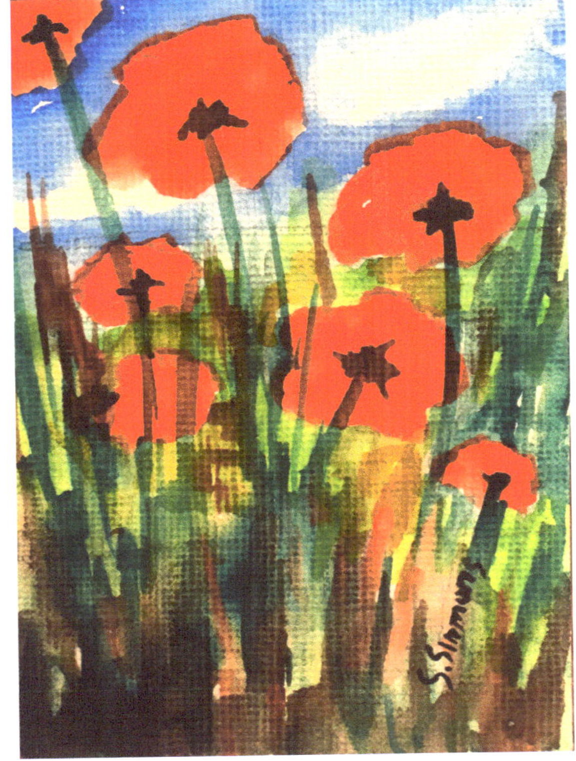

Little Red Flower (above), 2021
Acrylic on board, 6" x 8"

Little Poppy Dance (right), 2018
Acrylic on paper, 2" x 3"

Dance!

The music is inside of you

Listen, feel it, move to it

Dance and you can

Free yourself

And set yourself believing

That you can fly together

With wings that fill the sky

Dancer, 2021
Acrylic on canvas, 10" x 20"

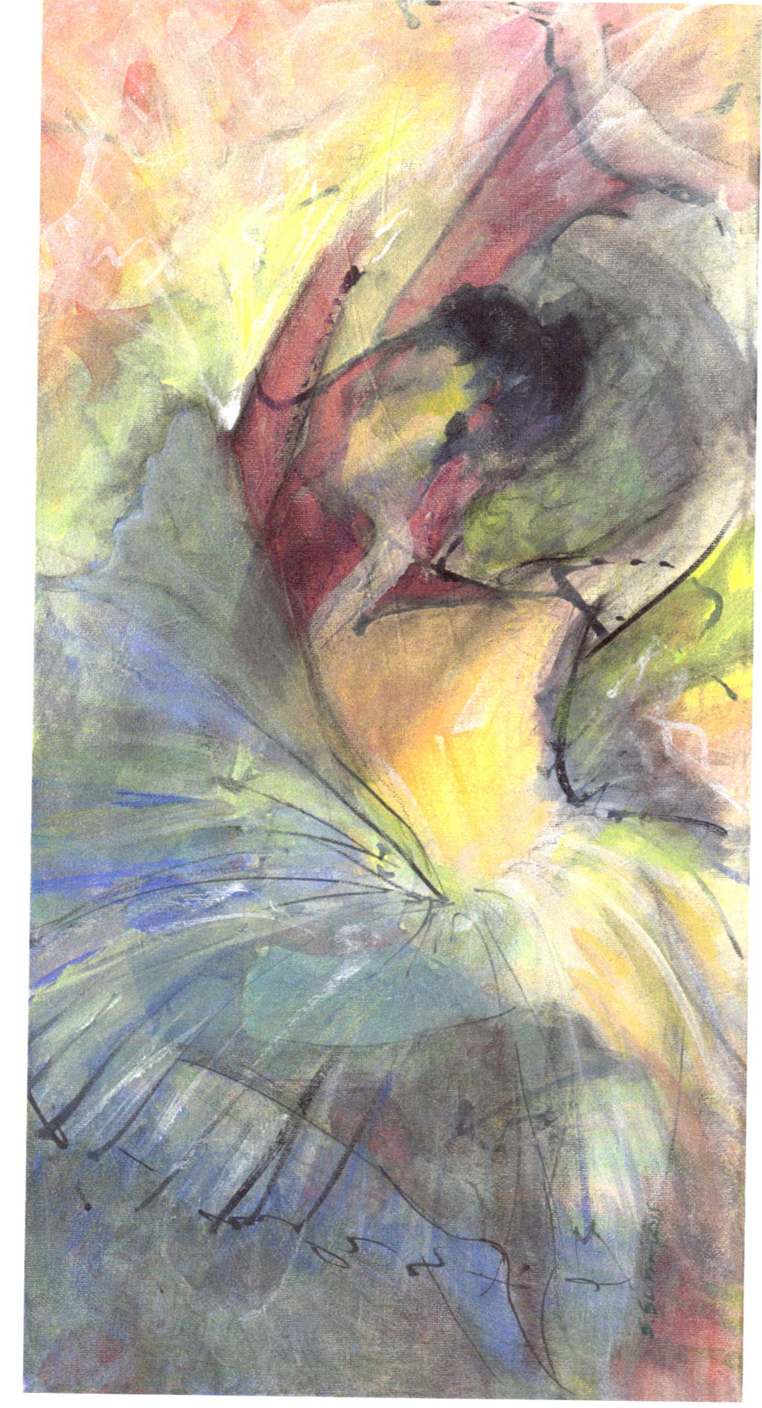

Filters

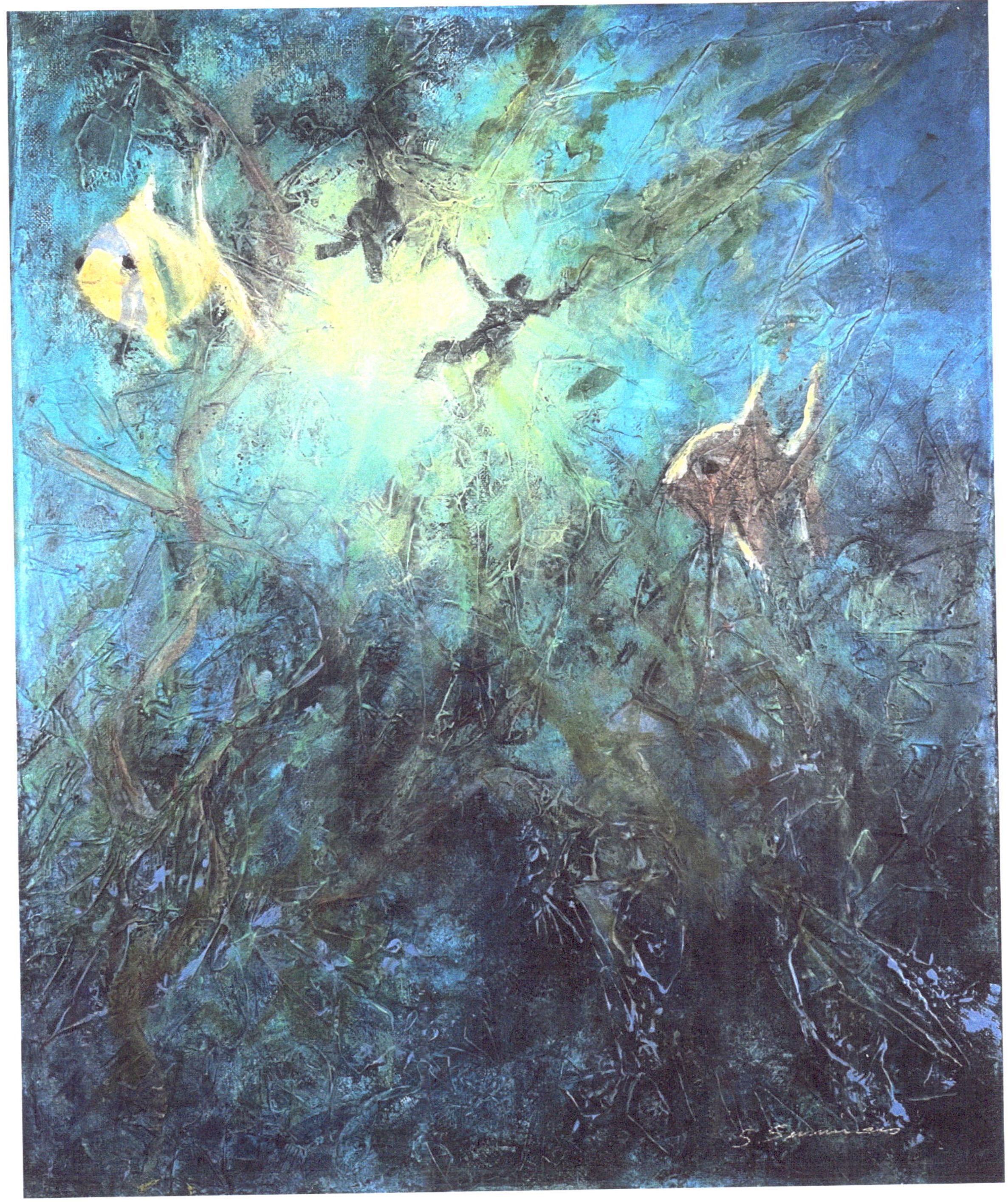

Ocean Dreams, 2022
Acrylic on canvas, 16" x 20"

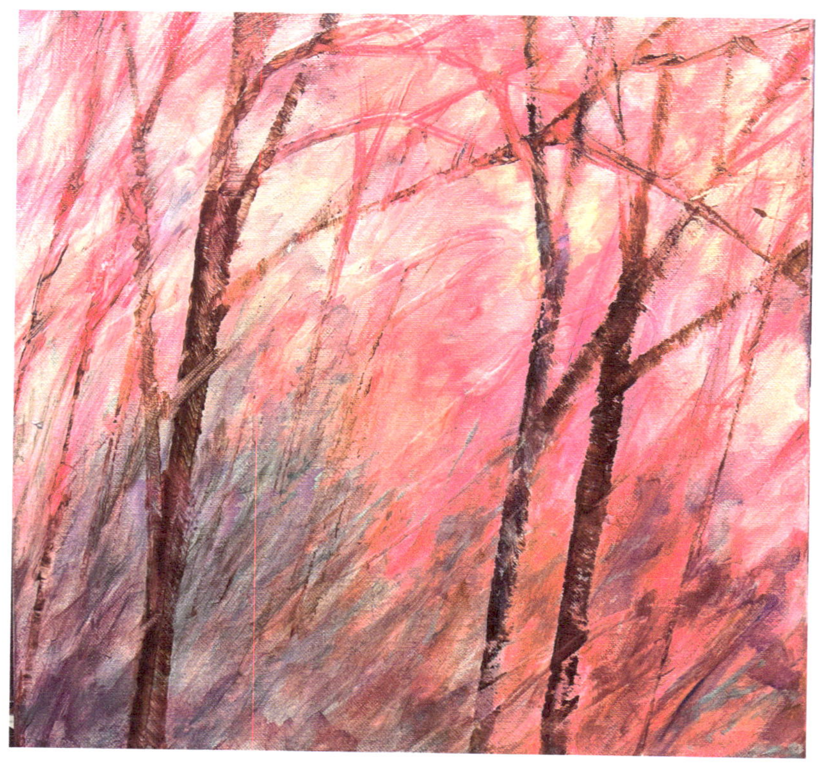

...I find new filters
in my life
and change
my point of view!

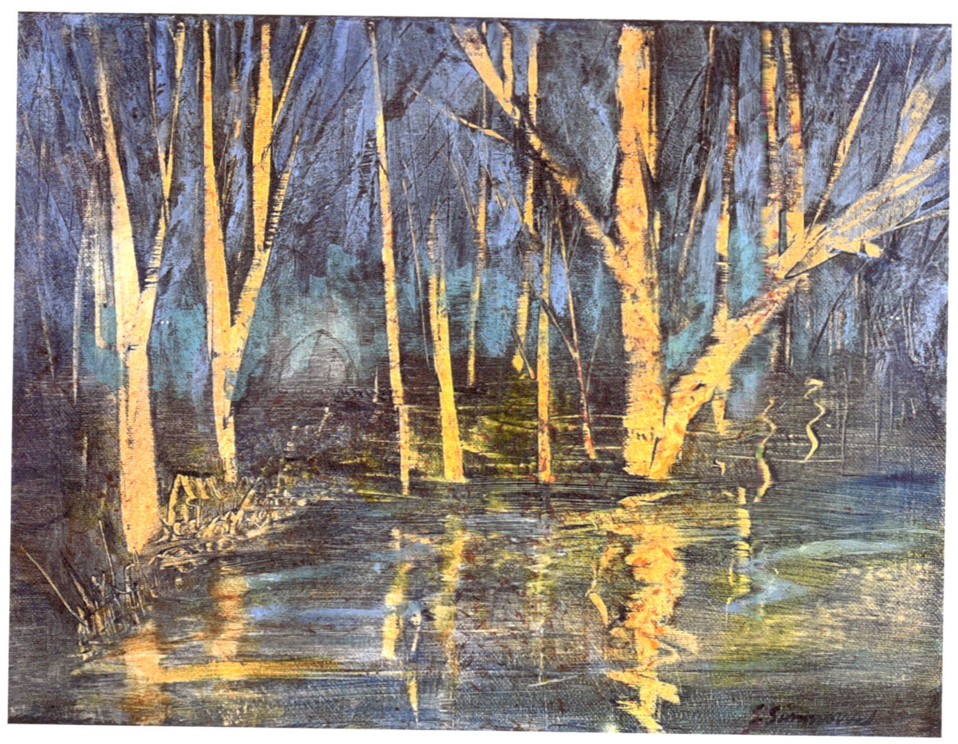

Rose-Colored Glasses (left), 2021
Acrylic on canvas, 14" x 14

Swamp Splendor (right), 2023
Acrylic on canvas, 11" x 14"

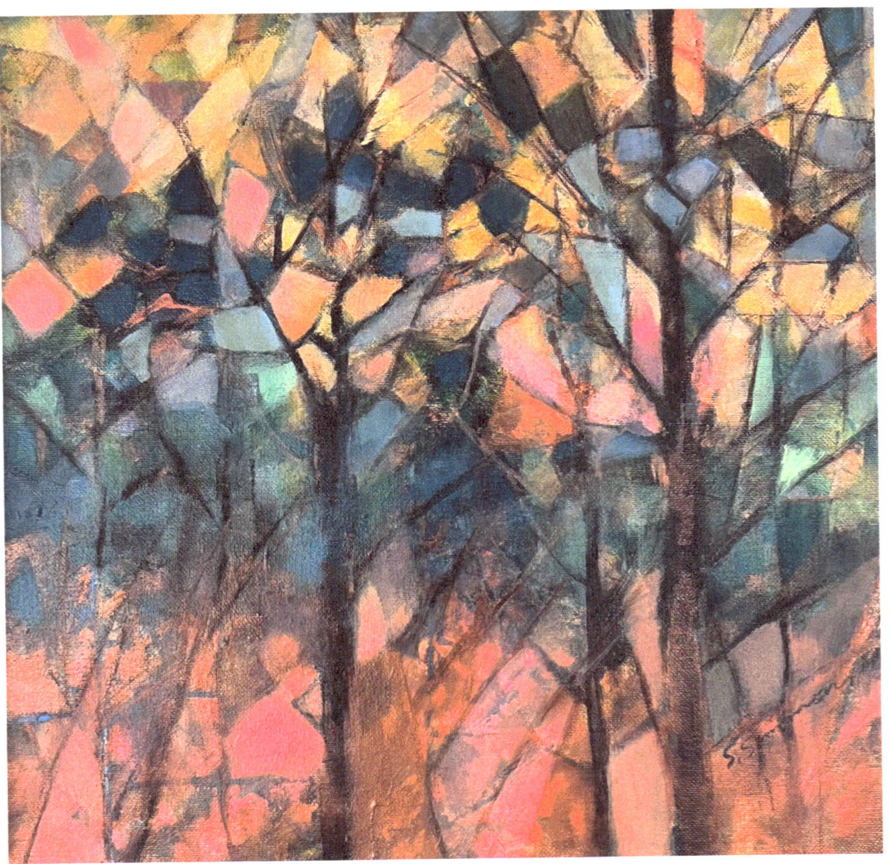

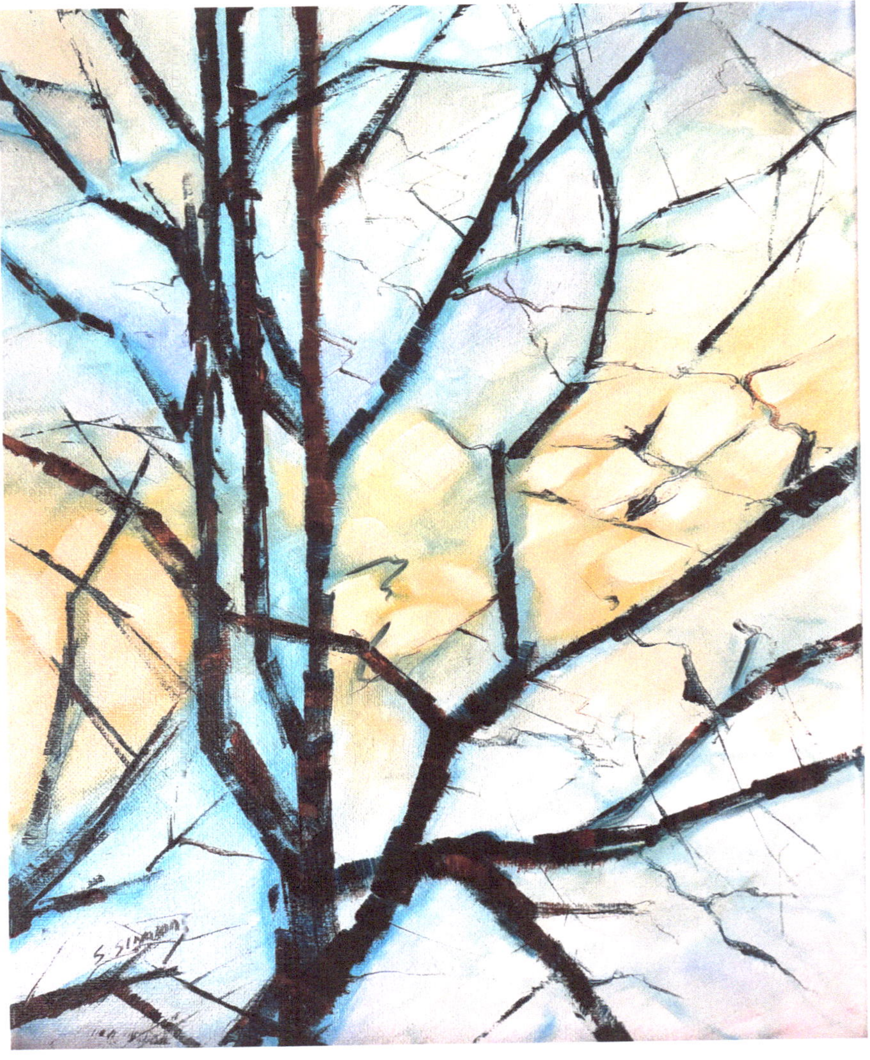

Patterns are predictable

I know what to expect

The rhythms dance within my soul

They help me see what's next

Kaleidoscope Trees (left), 2022
Acrylic on canvas, 14" x 14"

Cathedral Sky (right), 2021
Oil on canvas, 11" x 14"

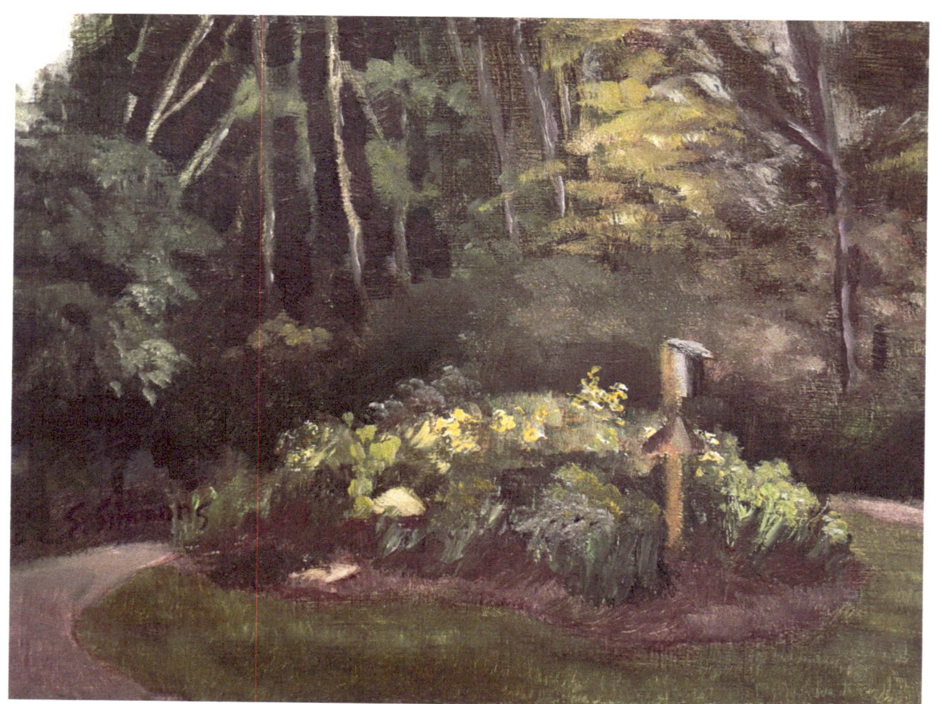

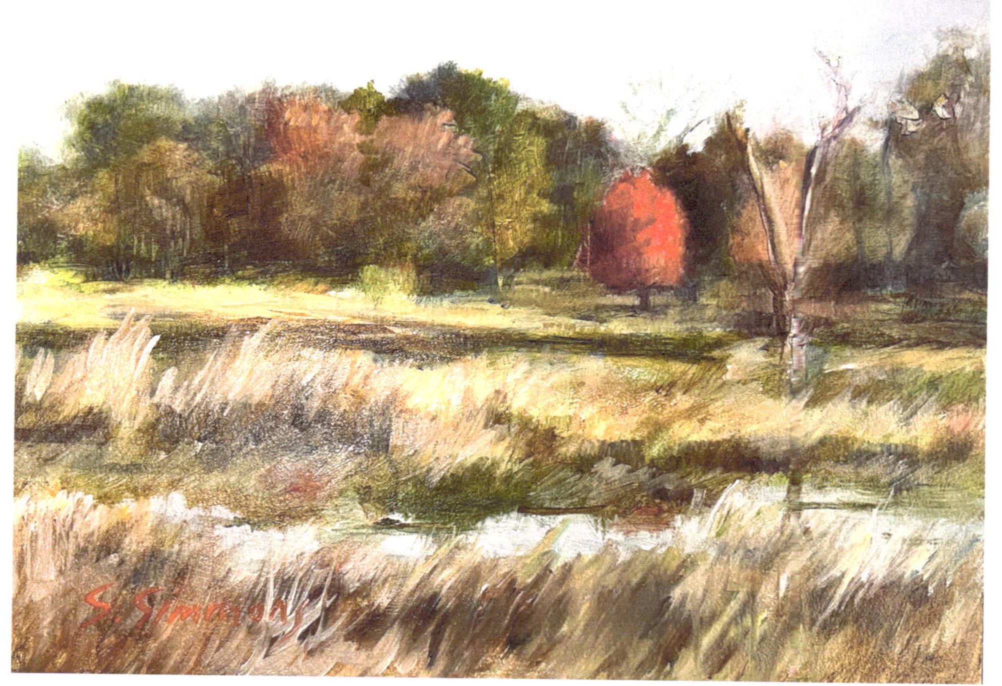

Bumble -Pye (above), 2024
Acrylic on hardboard, 5" x 7"

Blue Heron Overlook in Fall (right), 2022
Oil on board, 6" x 8"

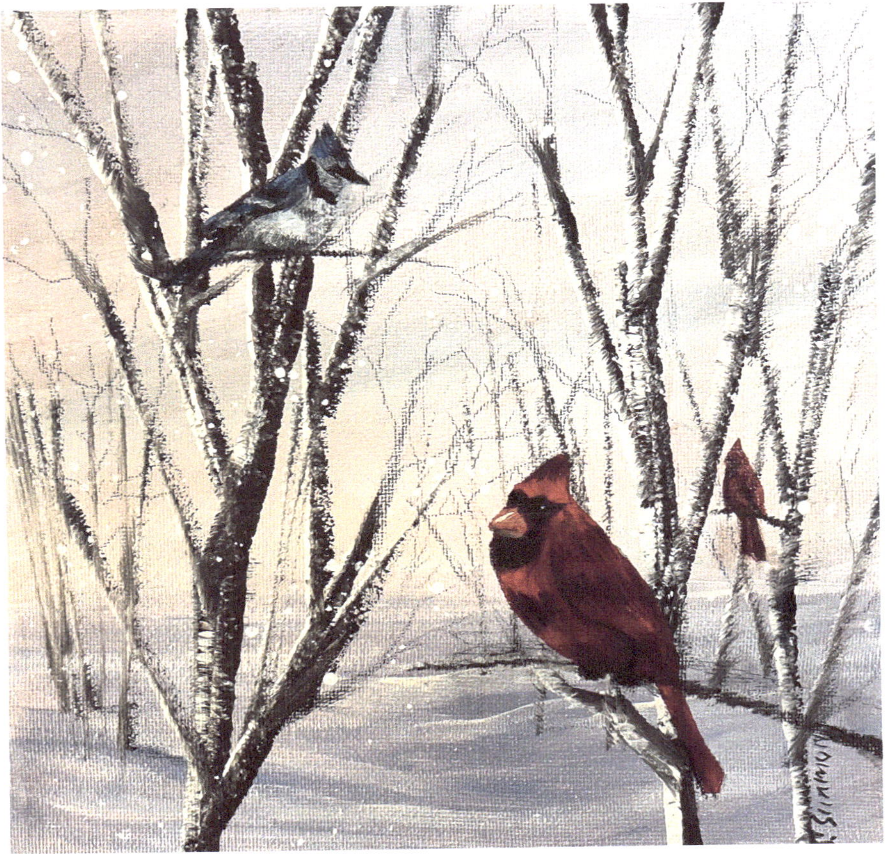

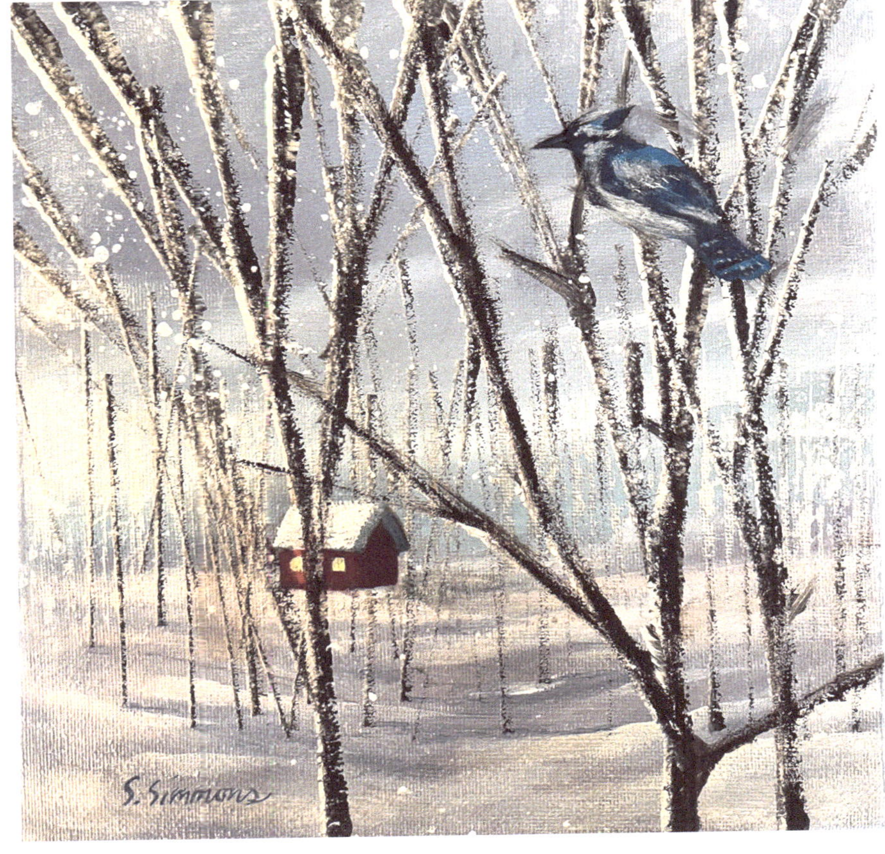

Holidays, unlike other days

Reflect the seasons past

Or mark new starting points to love

And new memories to last

Holiday series, 2021
Acrylic on canvas, 8" x 8"

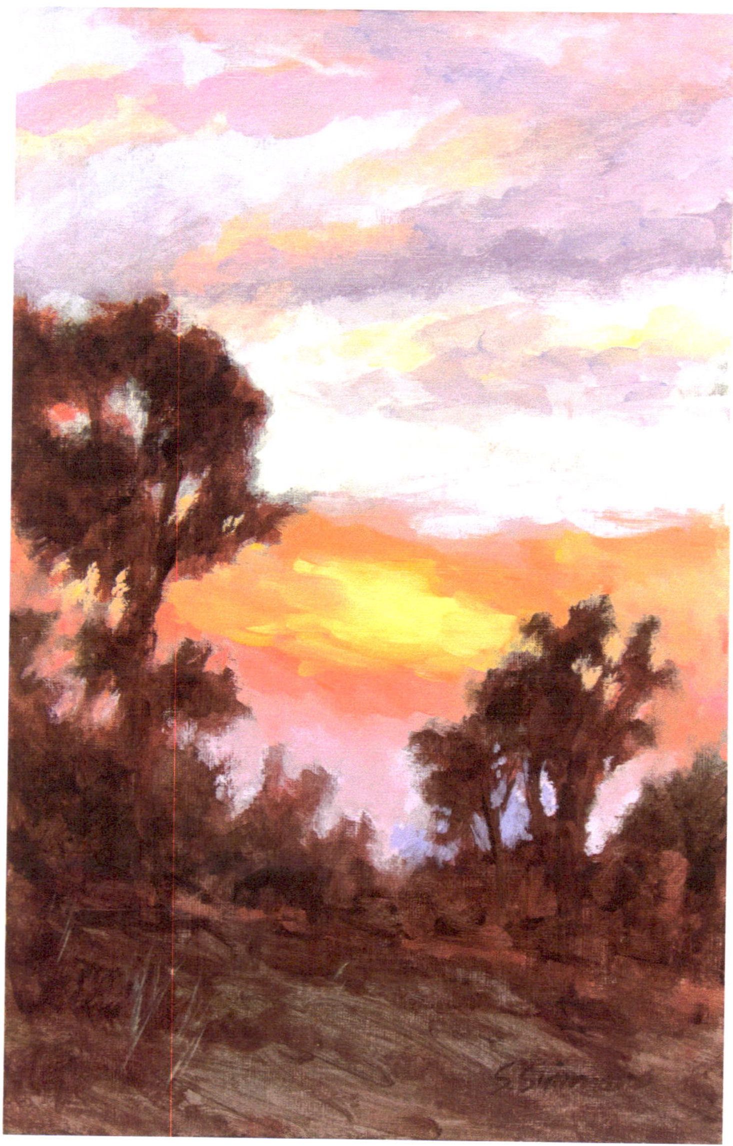

Closing the Day, (above), 2022
Acrylic on board, 9" x 15"

Sandhill Serenade (right), 2022
Acrylic on board, 9" x 15"

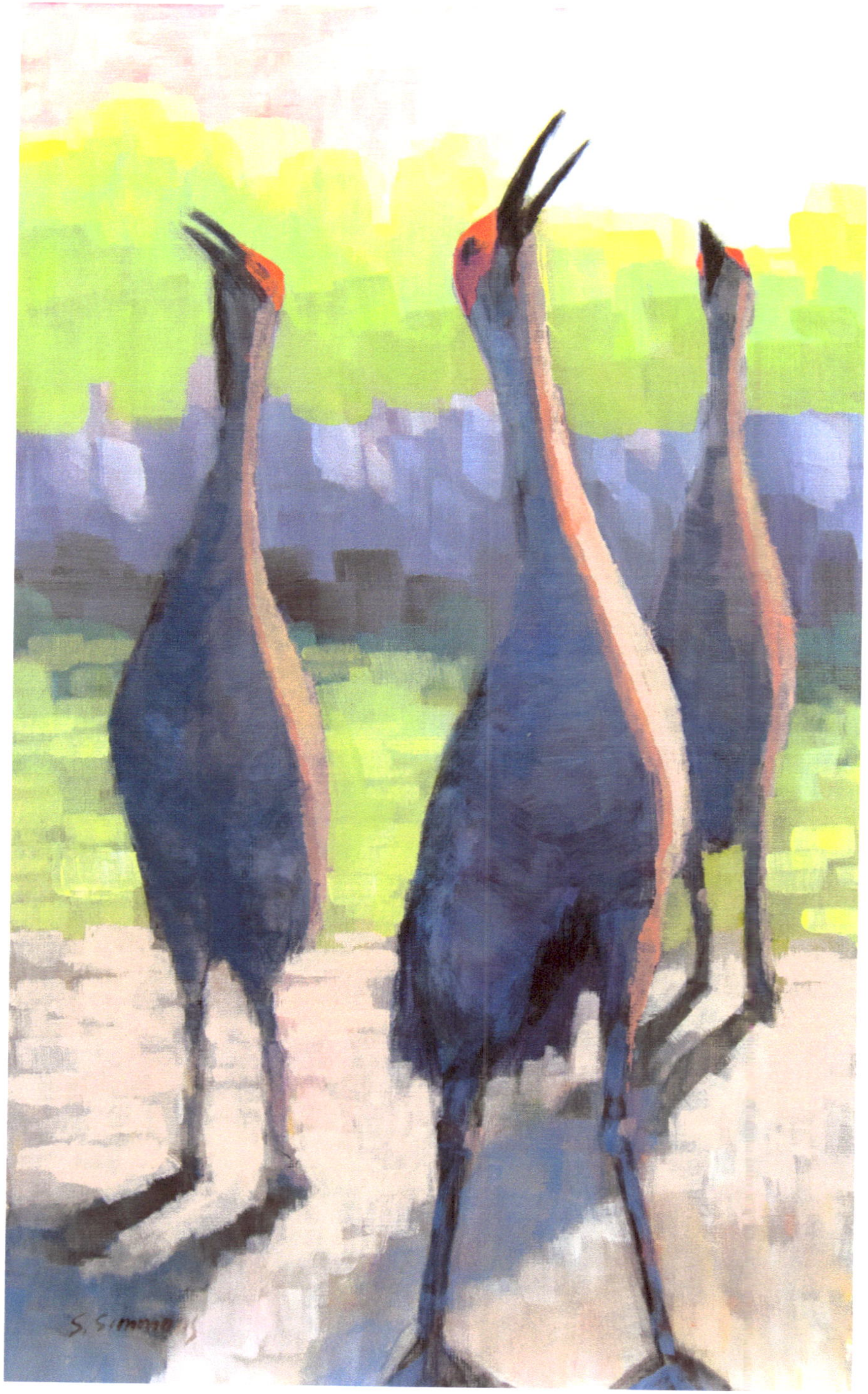

Facing Love

Soft and warm are gentle eyes

A friendly welcome start

A place to rest and feel again

With a topsy-turvy heart

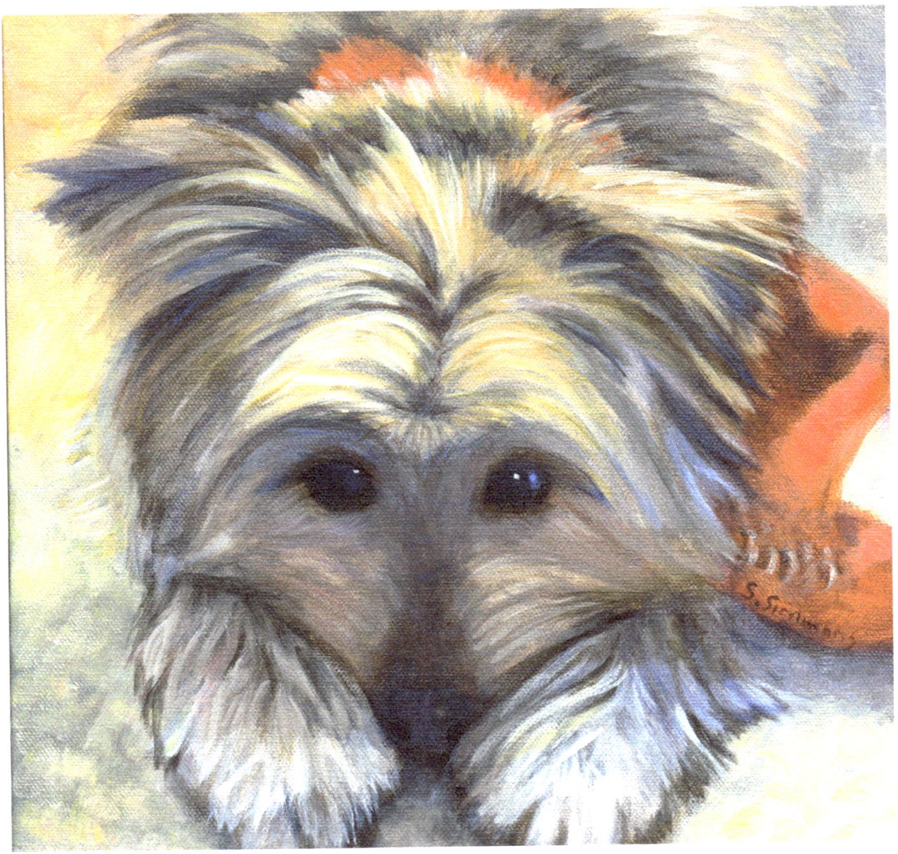

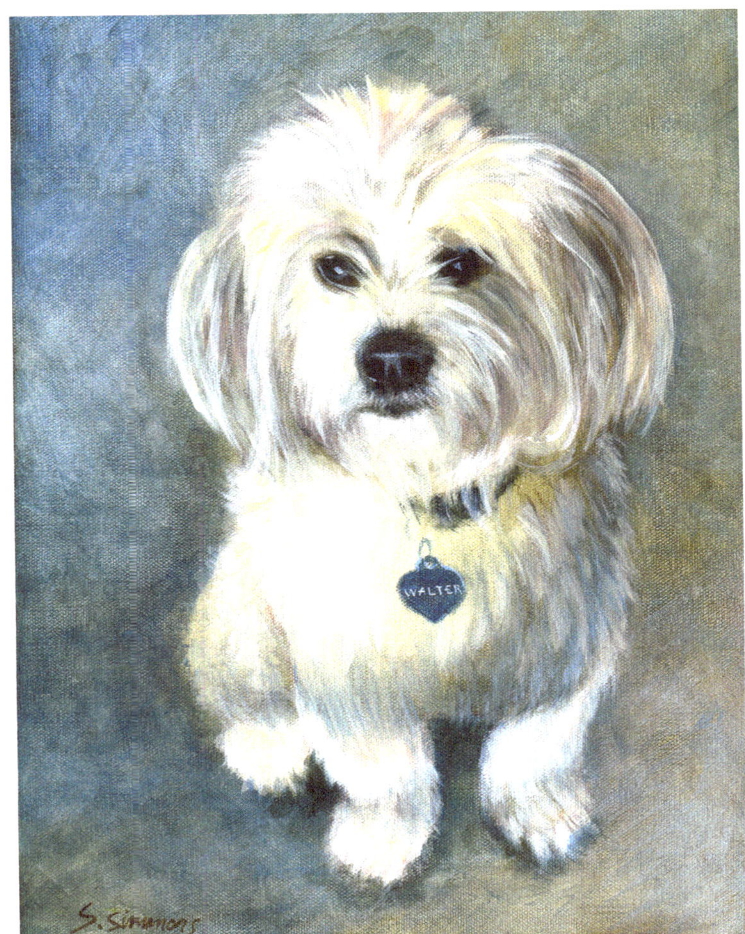

...They soothe me and remind me

With their silent gaze in view,

Reflecting love I find within,

To rise and start anew

Tig (above), 2018
Acrylic on canvas, 12" x 12"

Walter (right), 2018
Acrylic on canvas, 9" x 12"

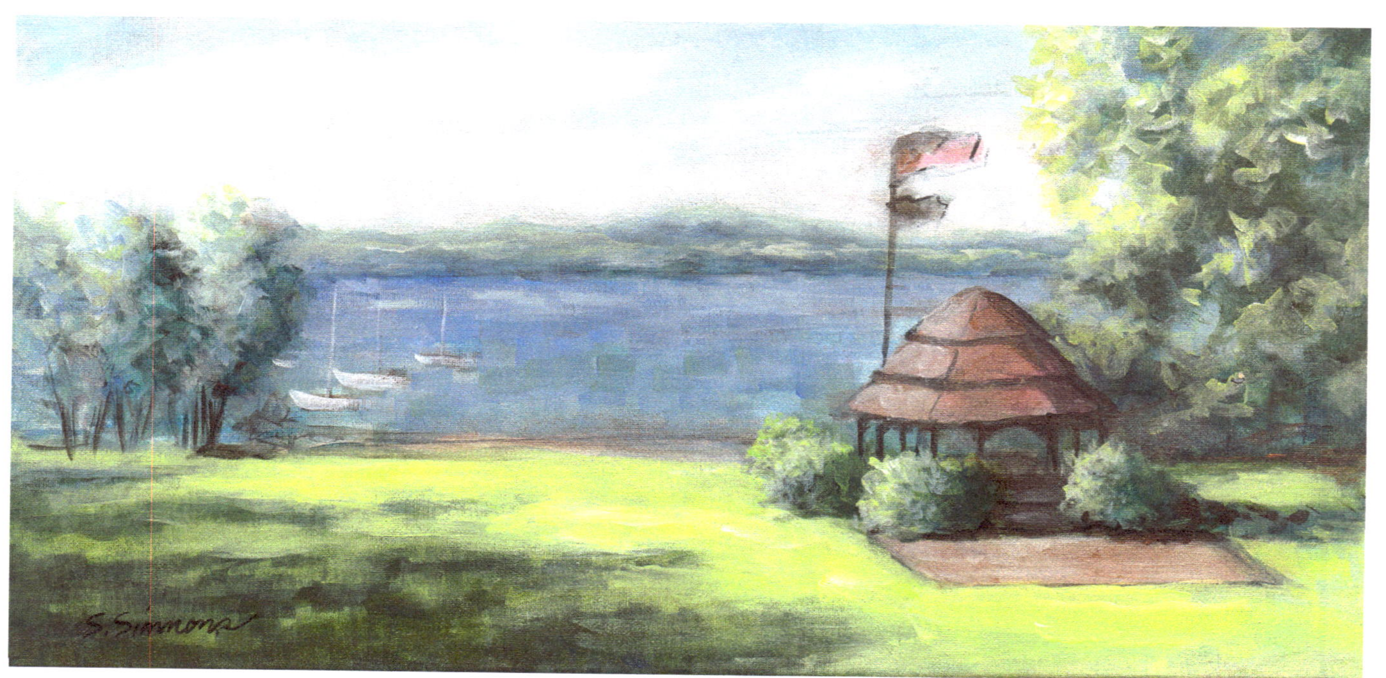

Lakewood Love

Hartley Park Then (above), 2020
Acrylic on canvas, 10" x 20"

Hartley Park Chill (right), 2024
Acrylic on canvas, 10" x 20"

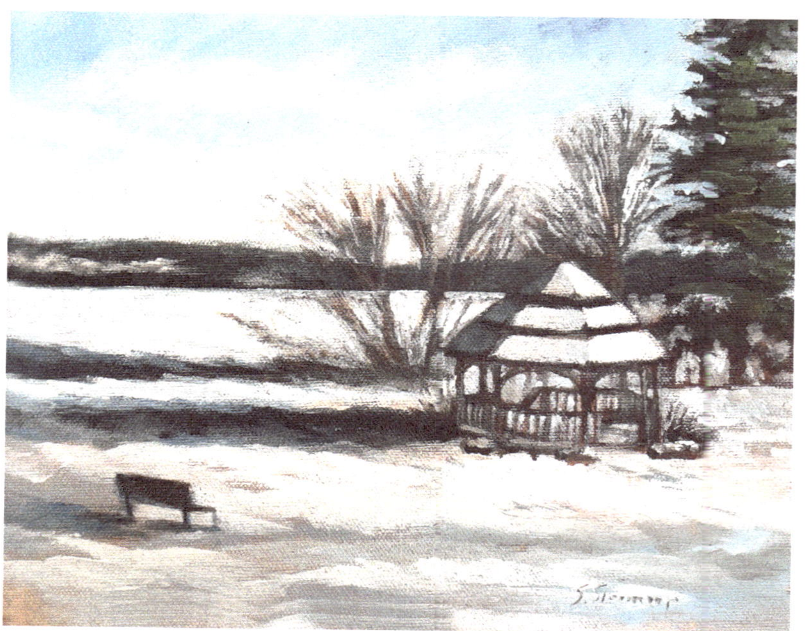

The trees outside protect me
They whisper in the wind
I listen to them with my heart
They ground me once again

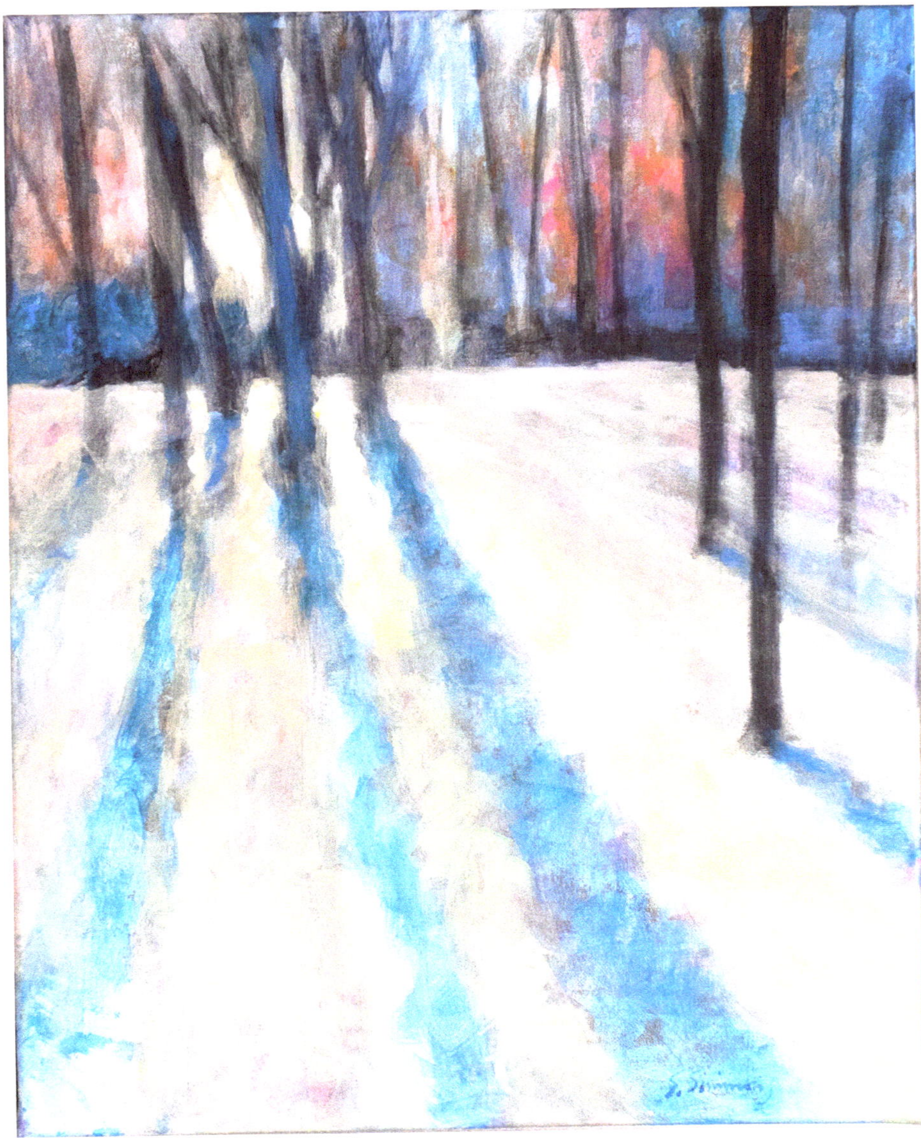

Shadowplay (above), 2022
Acrylic on canvas, 16" x 20"

Robyn's Hideaway (right), 2022
Acrylic on canvas, 14" x 18"

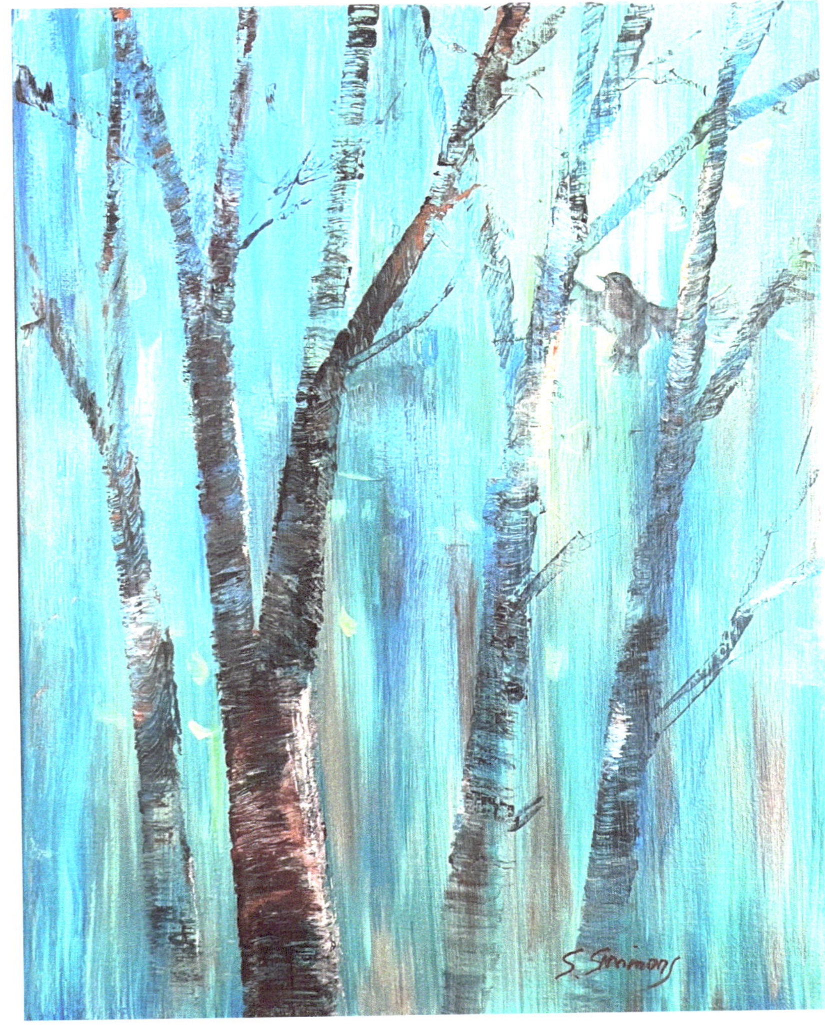

Imagine

I travel to another place

In the colors of my mind

They show up in just minutes

As if self-designed

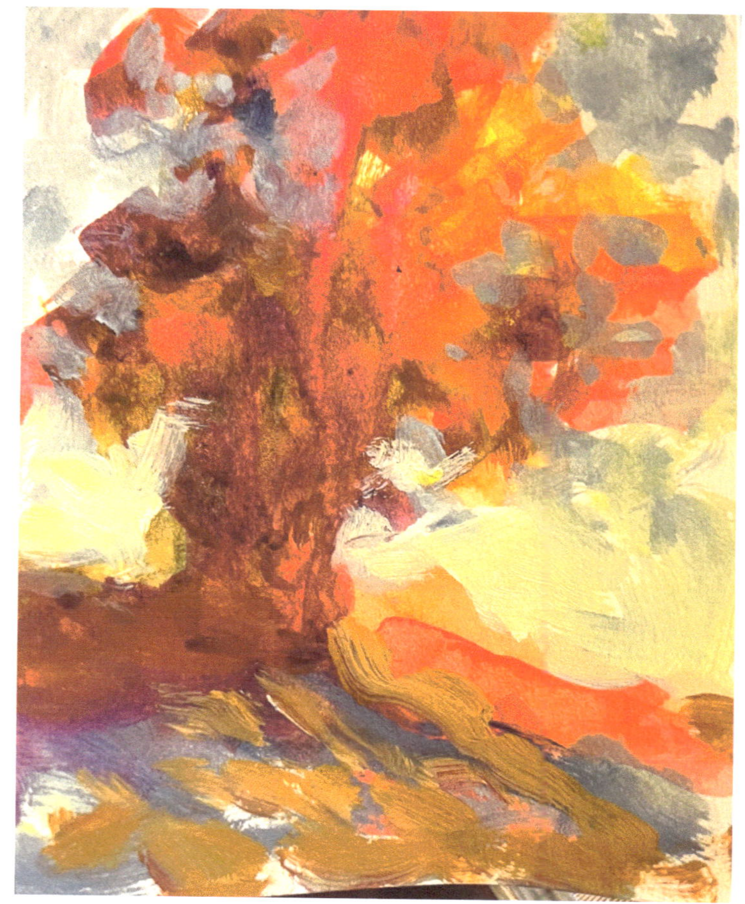

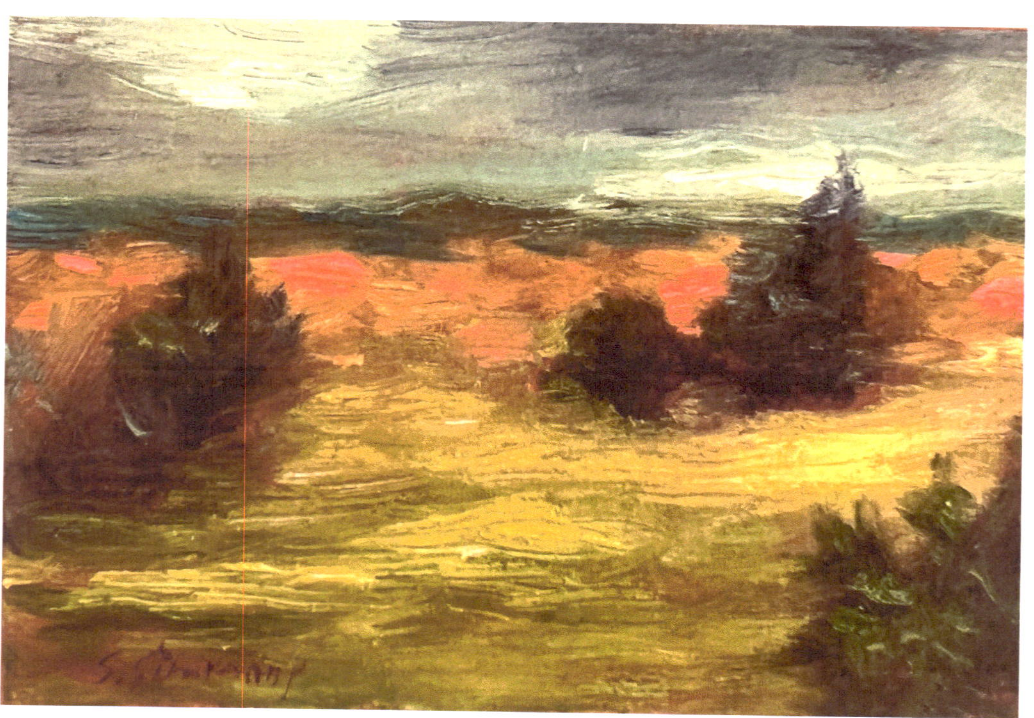

Chautauqua Overlook (left), 2024
Oil on paper, 2" x 3"

Golden Foliage (above), 2024
Oil on paper, 2" x 3"

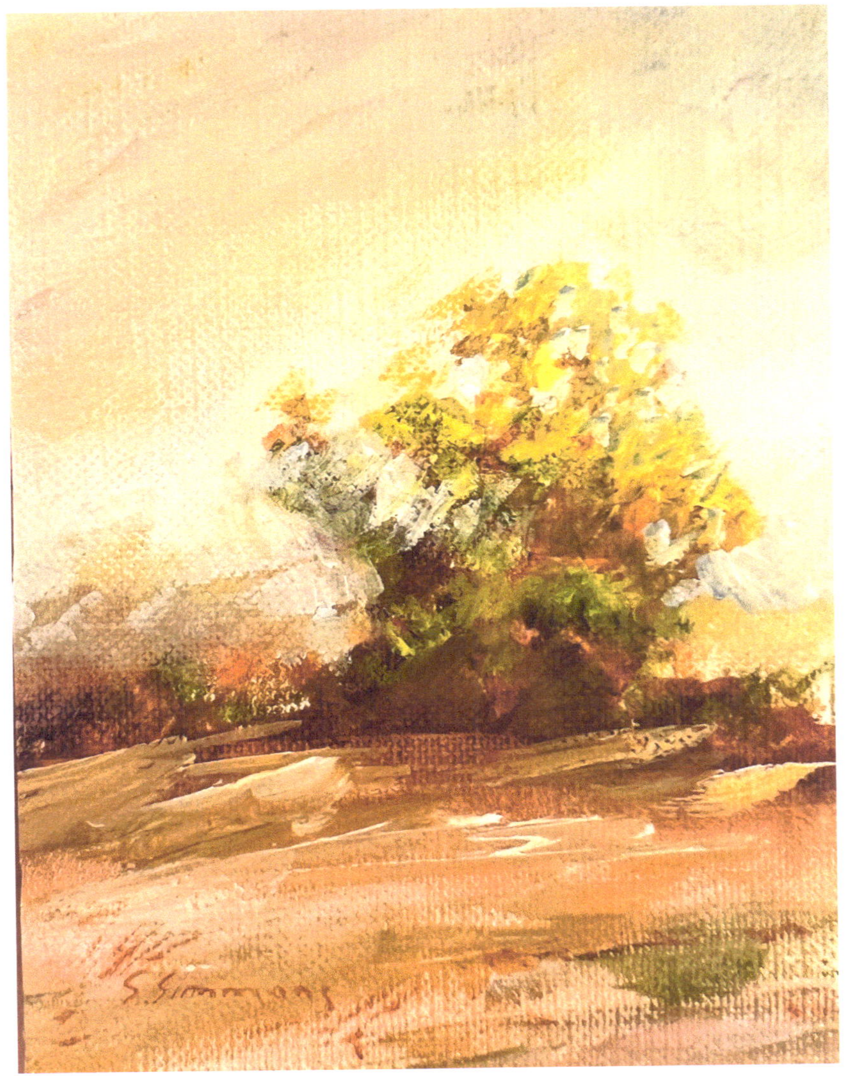

The
Lighter Side

Peaceful breezes whisper by

Beneath a soft and gentle sky

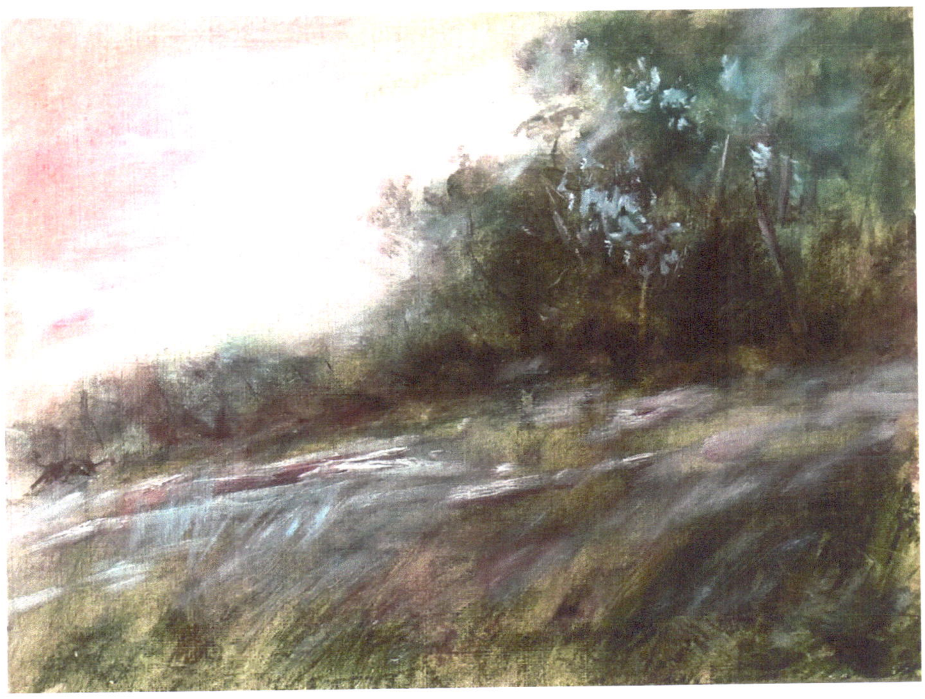

Summer Bliss (above), 2024
Oil on paper, 3.5" x 4"

Cool Spring Morning (right), 2020
Oil on paper, 9" x 12"

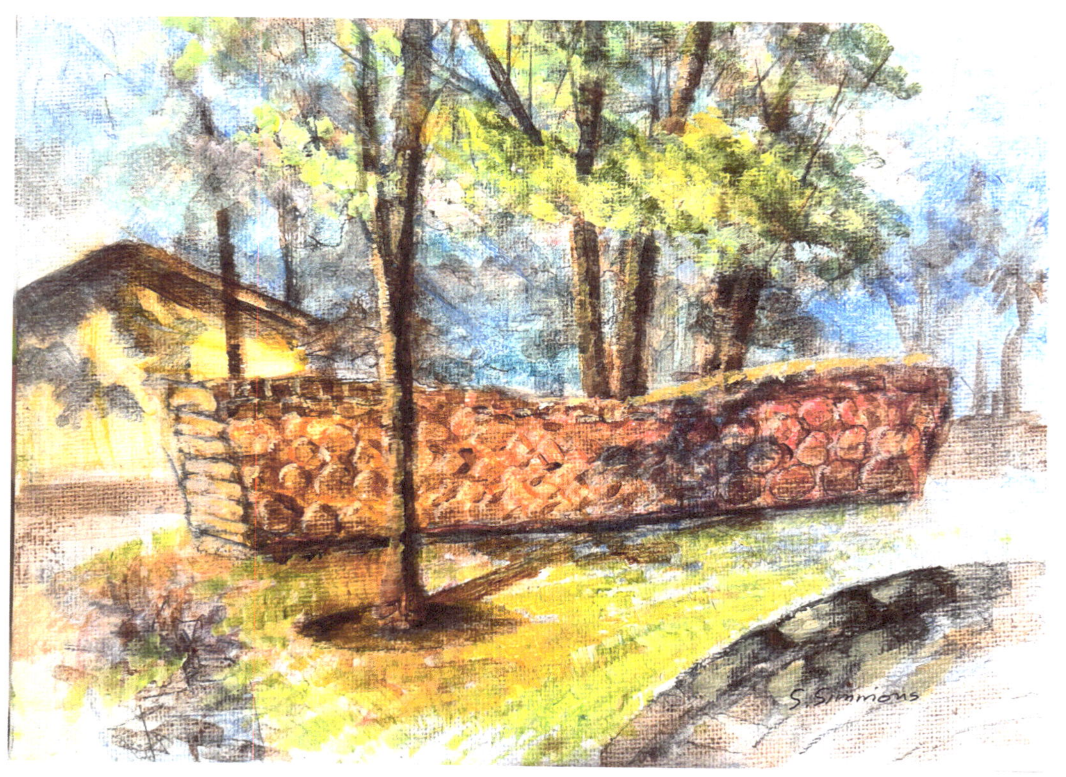

P l a y

A woodpile it seems

Little ship of dreams

Take me for a little ride

Across the great blue oceans-wide

Mark's Woodpile (above), 2023
Acrylic on board, 6" x 8"

Arkwright Haystacks (right), 2023
Oil on board, 6" x 8"

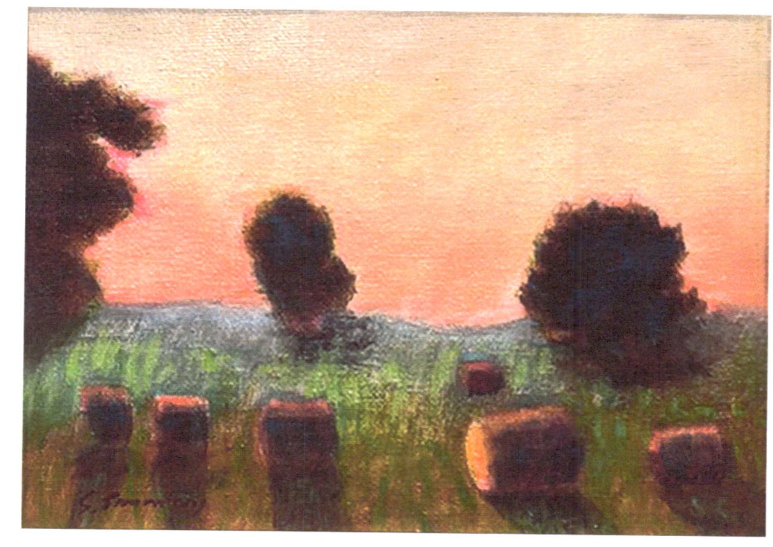

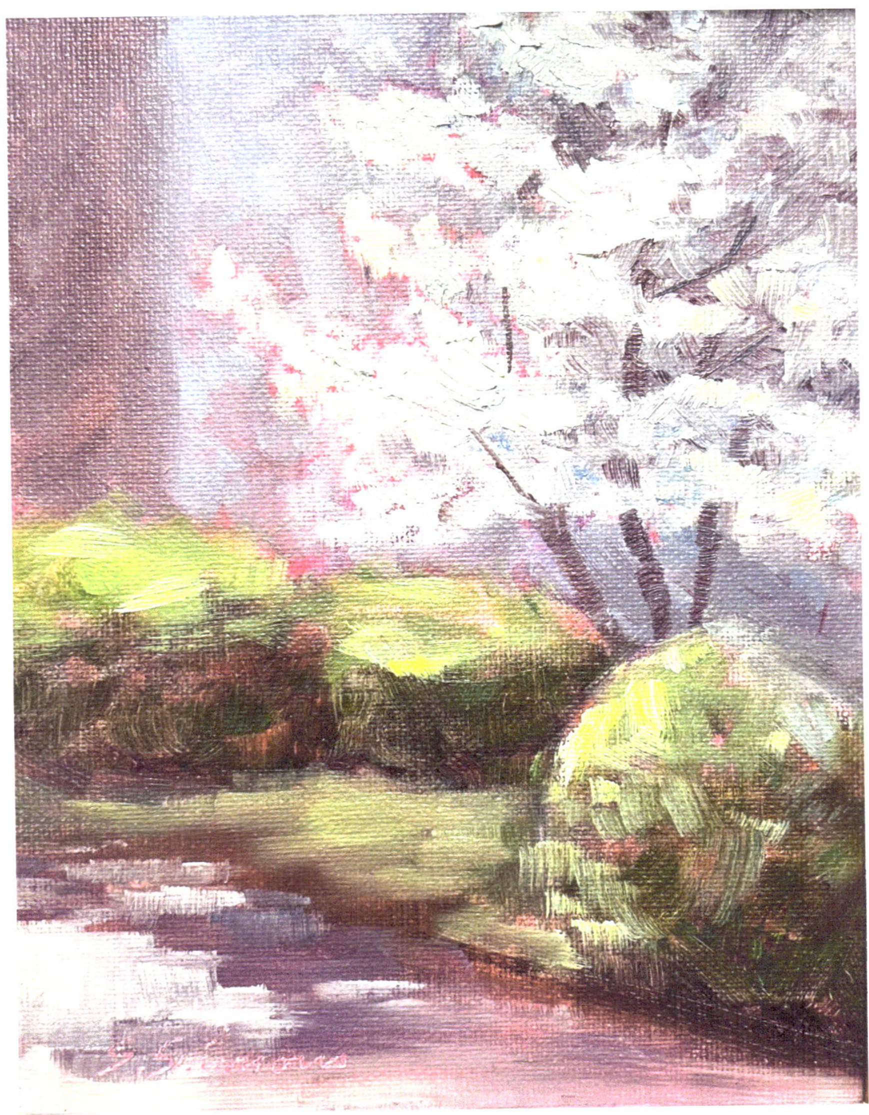

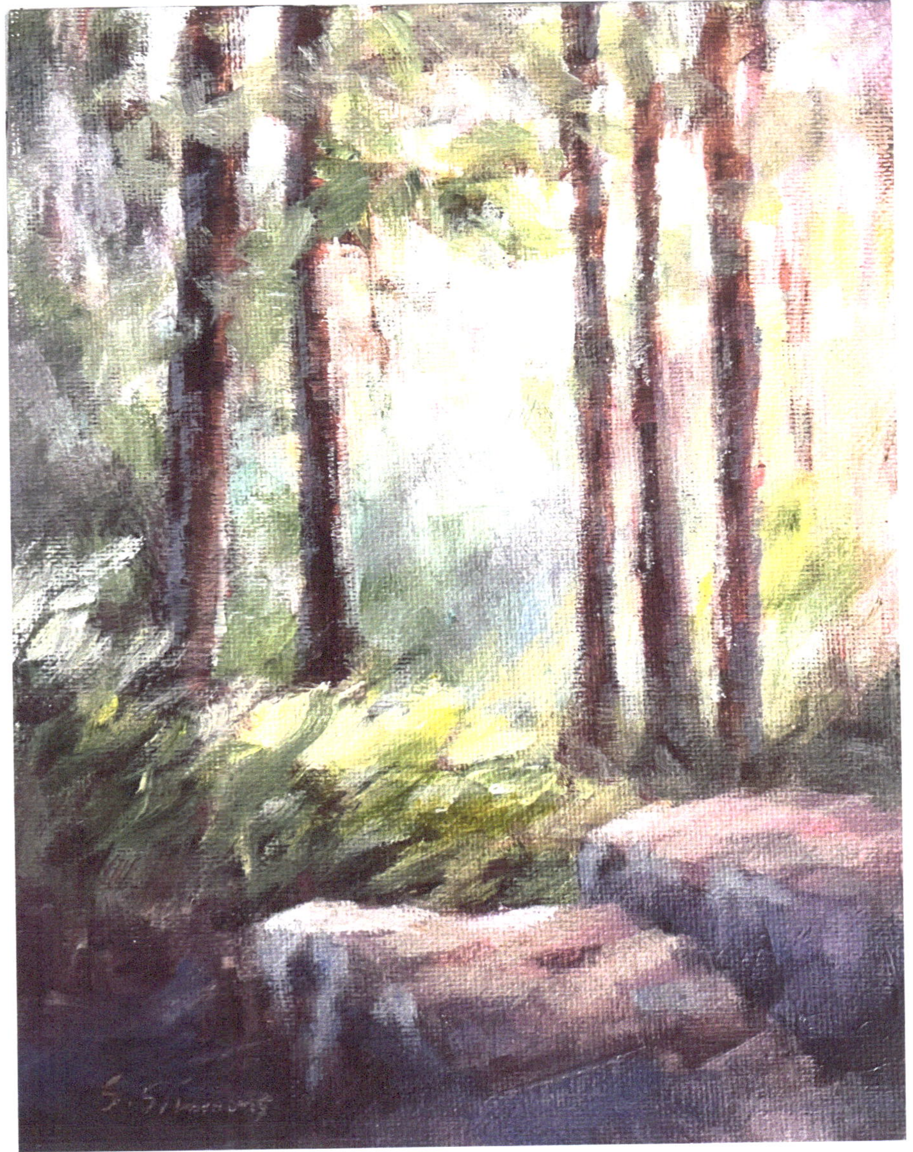

Hanna's Lavender Summer (above), 2023
Oil on board, 6" x 8"

Panama Rocks (right), 2023
Oil on board, 6" x 8"

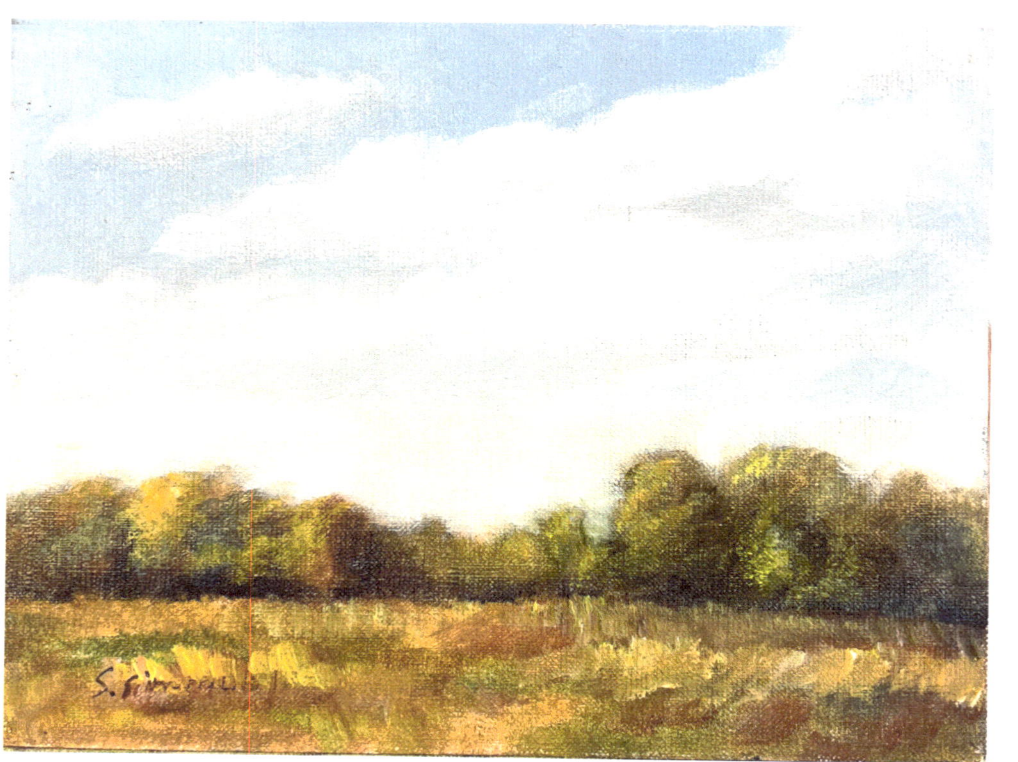

E X P A N D

Explore, Expand!

Surprise yourself

New places to embrace

Can be your ticket,

Your get-away

To your happy place!

A Golden Hour (above), 2023
Oil on board, 5" x 7"

Blue Heron Overlook (right), 2022
Oil on board, 6" x 8"
Winner-Oil/acrylic category - 2022 Roger Tory Peterson
Plein Air Festival

Erie through the Trees (facing page), 2023
Oil on board, 6" x 8"

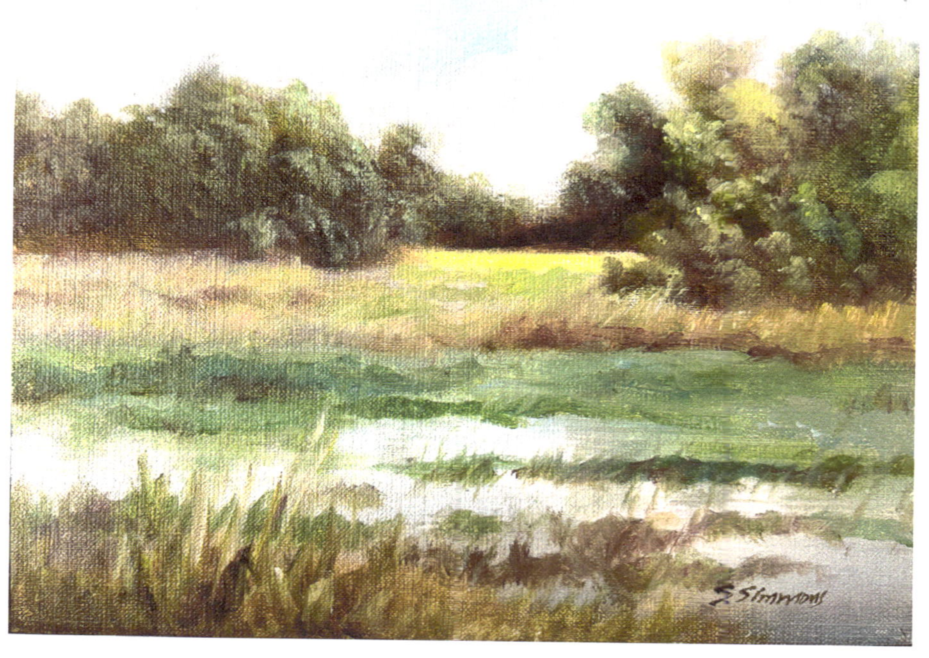

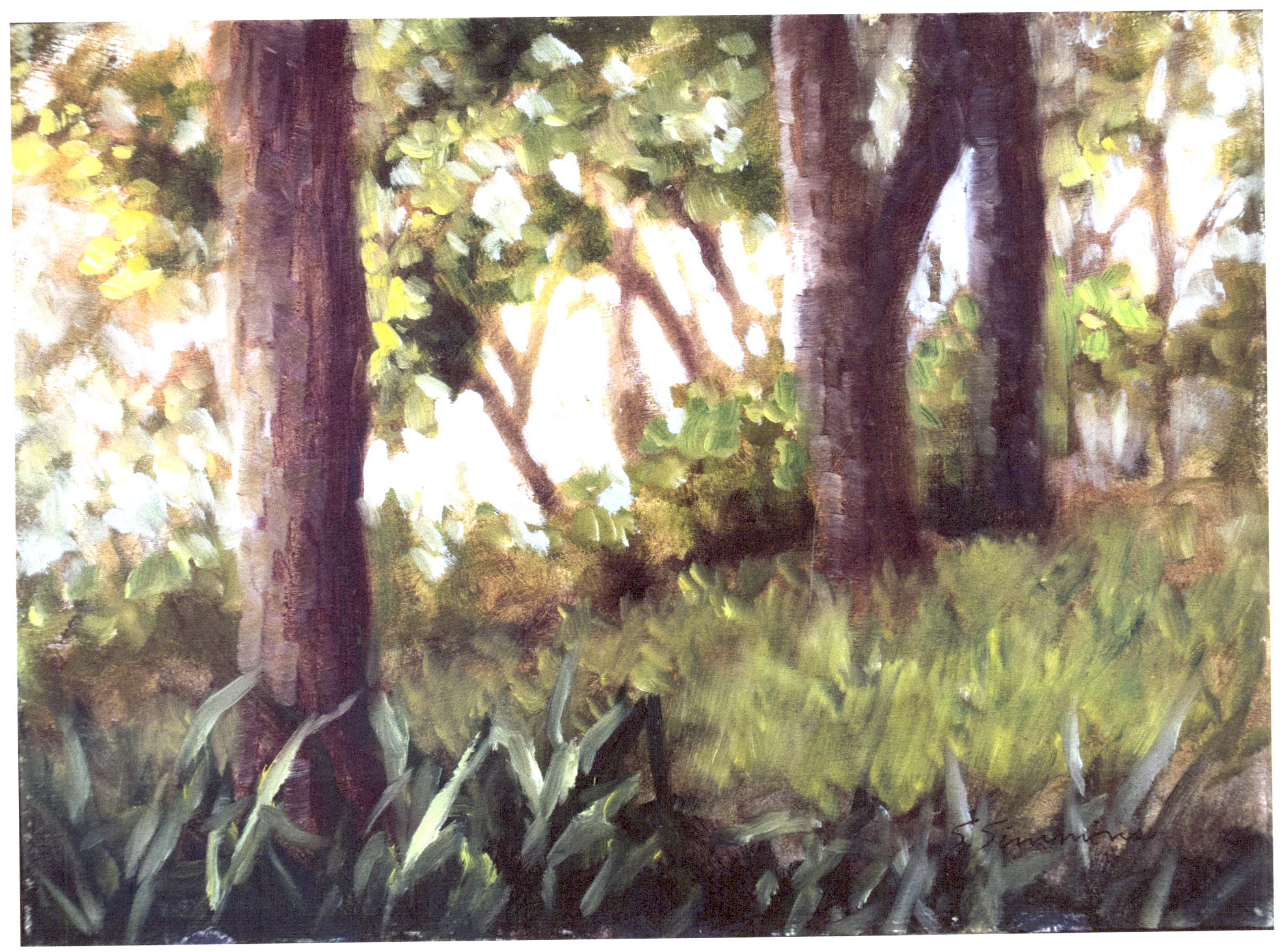

SIMPLIFY!

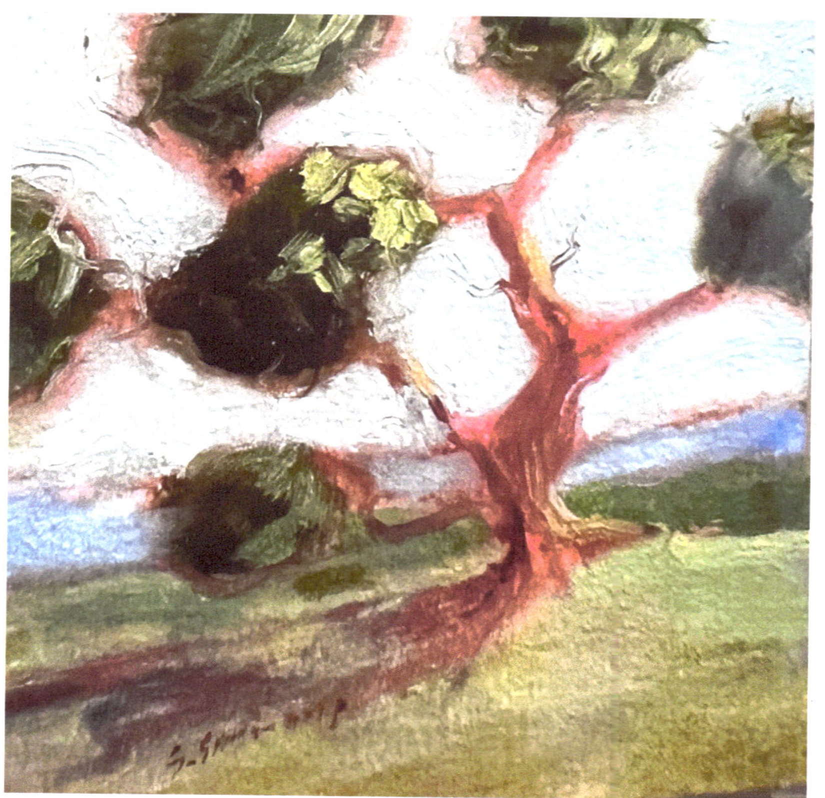

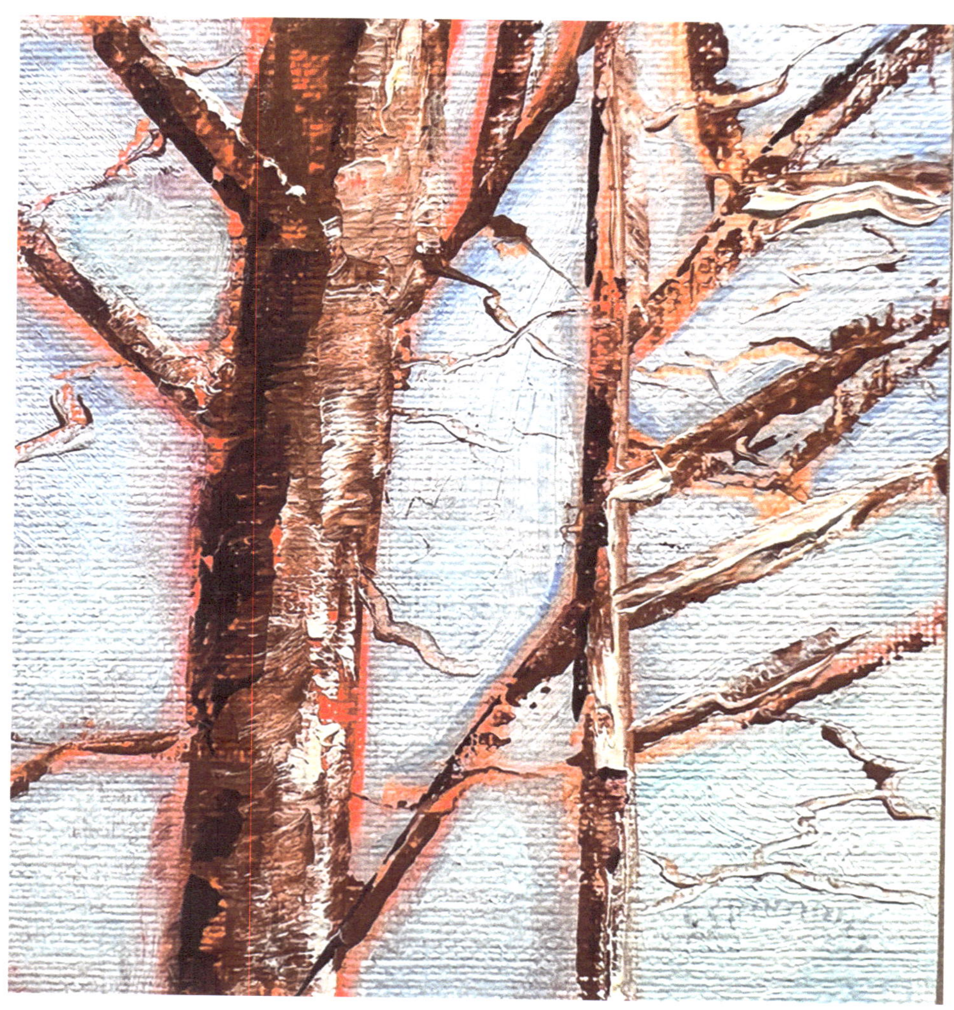

Branchy (left), 2021
Oil on archival paper, 3" x 3.5"

Simplicitree (above), 2022
Oil on archival paper, 3" x 3"

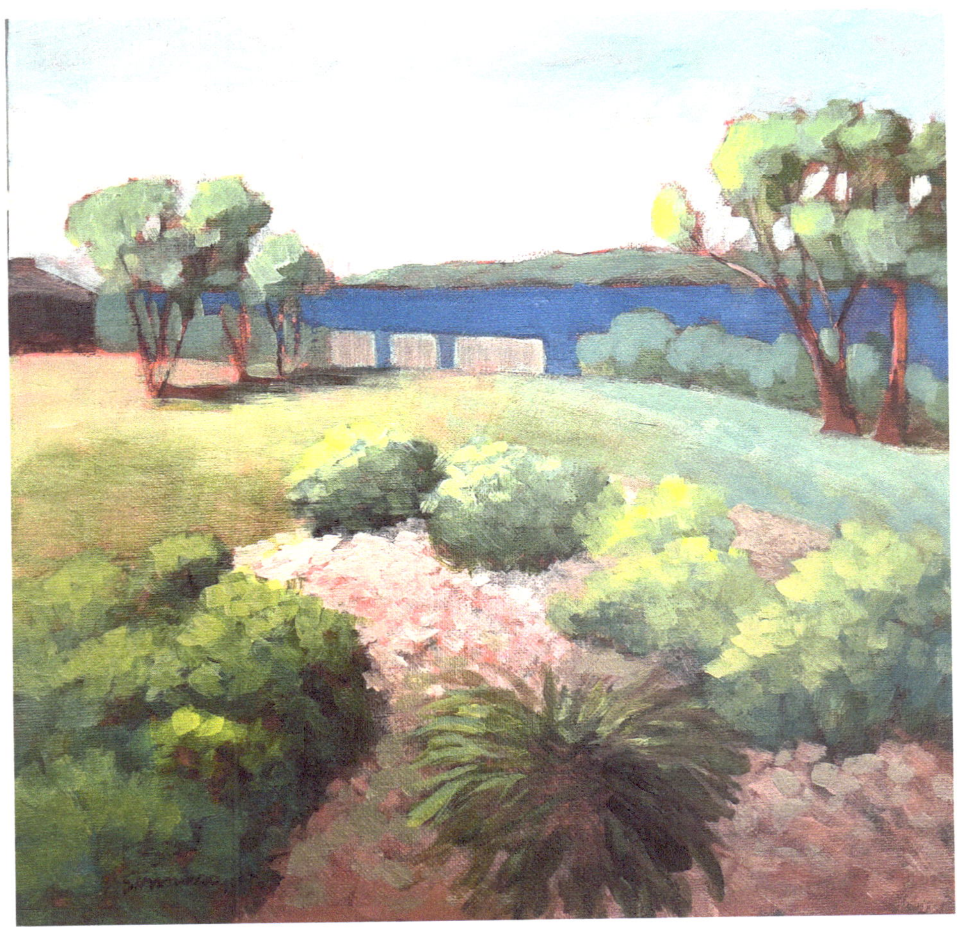

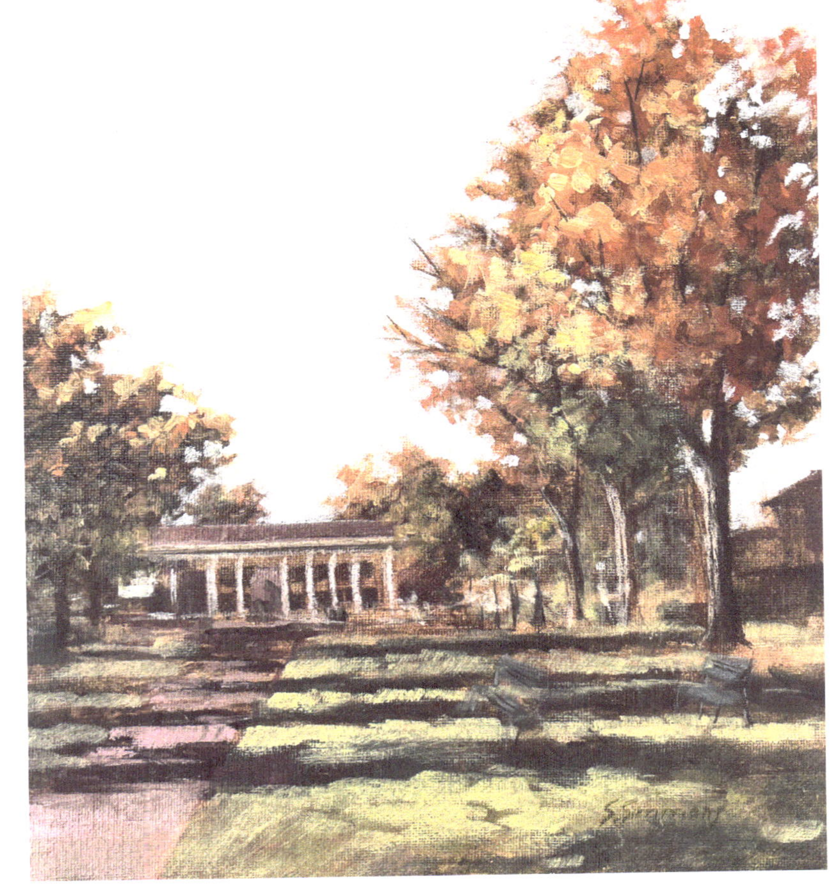

Hartley Park Heat (above), 2023
Oil on board, 12" x 12"

The Colonnade (right), 2023
Acrylic on board, 9" x 12"

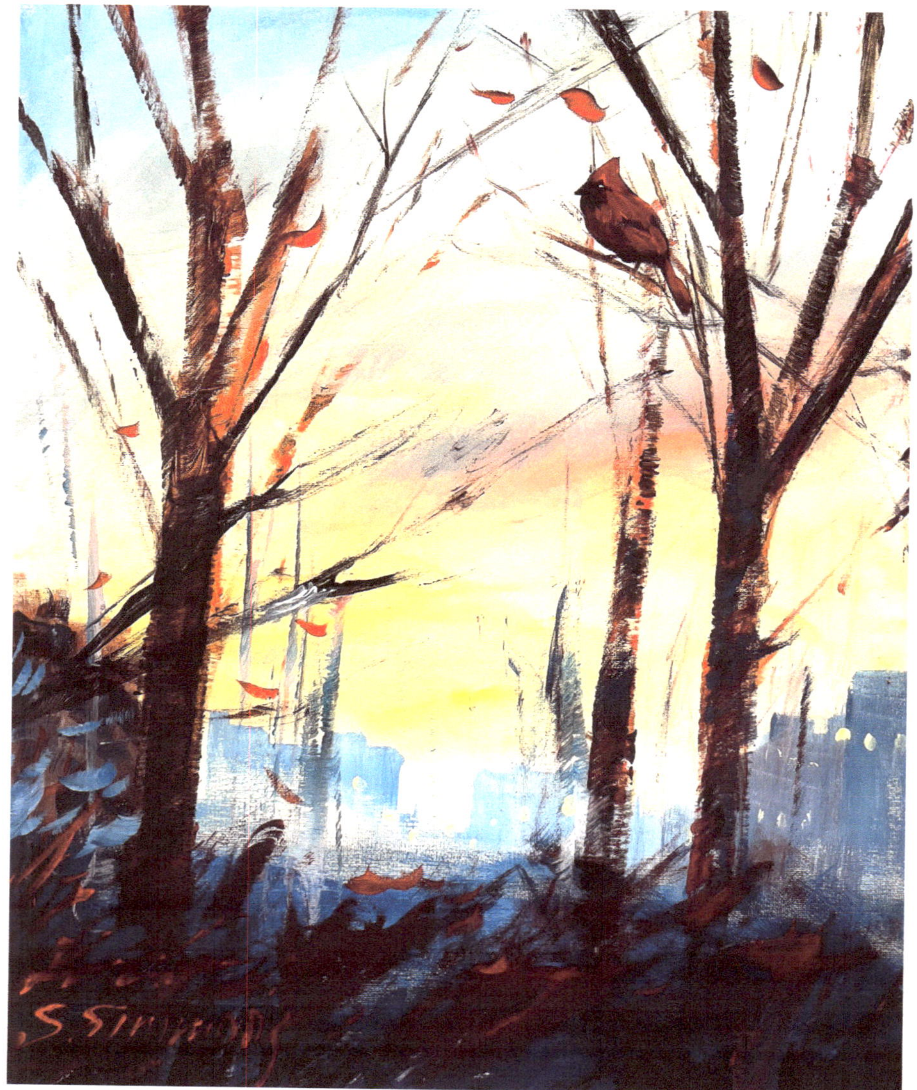

Dream

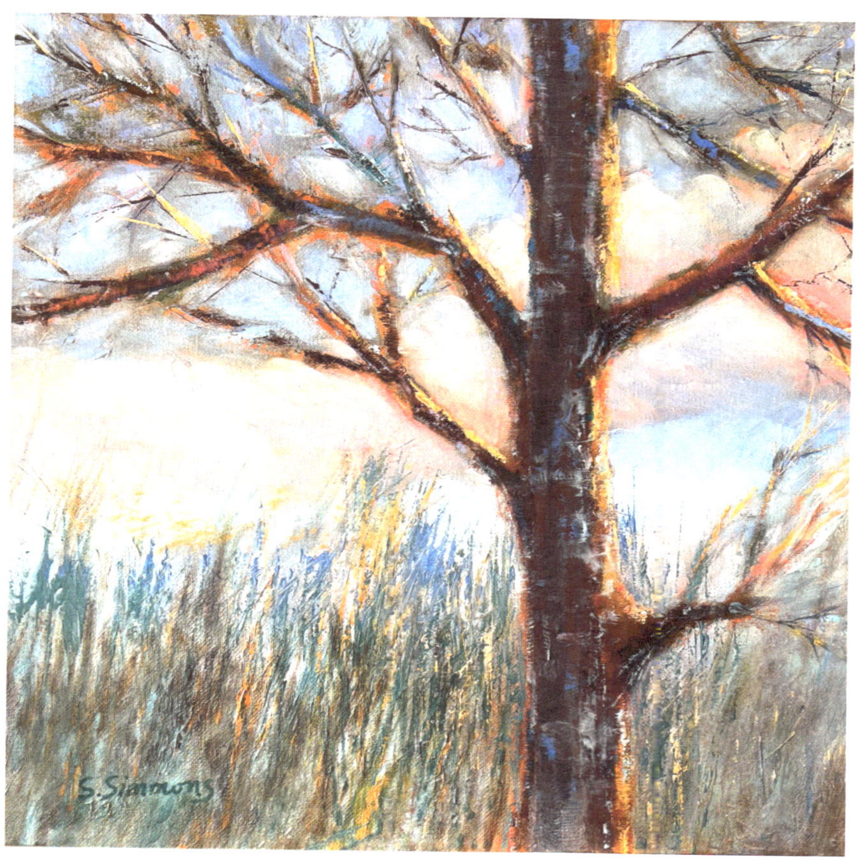

Seeing the Forest Through the Trees (above), 2024
Acrylic on canvas, 16" x 20"

Afterglow (right), 2021
Oil on canvas, 14" x 14"a

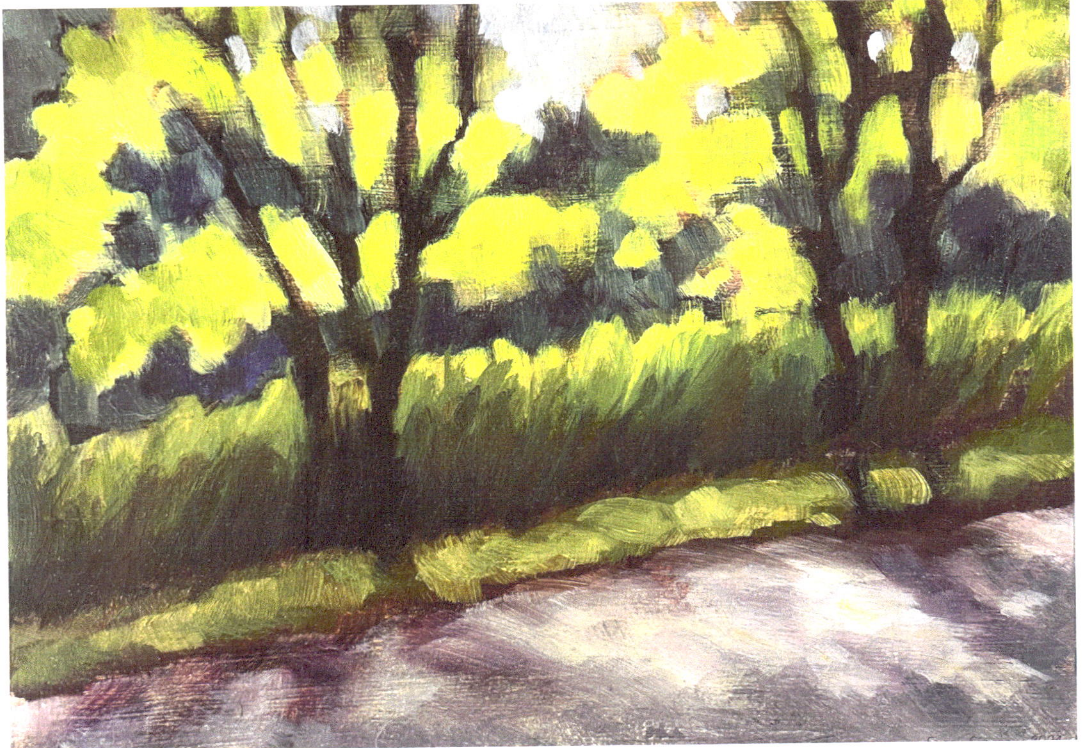

GLOW

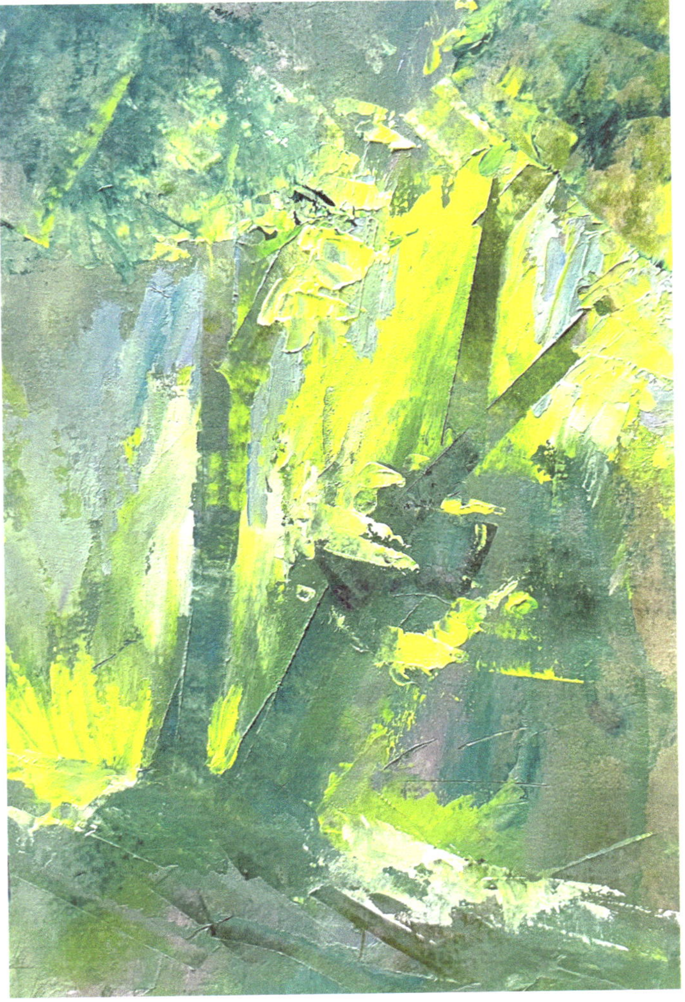

The trees that fill my space in time

Give breath of life on earth

They glow with the light of life itself

Continuing their upward climb!

Limon-Berry (above), 2024
Oil on board, 6" x 8"

Loose Chartreuse (right), 2024
Oil on paper, 3" x 4"

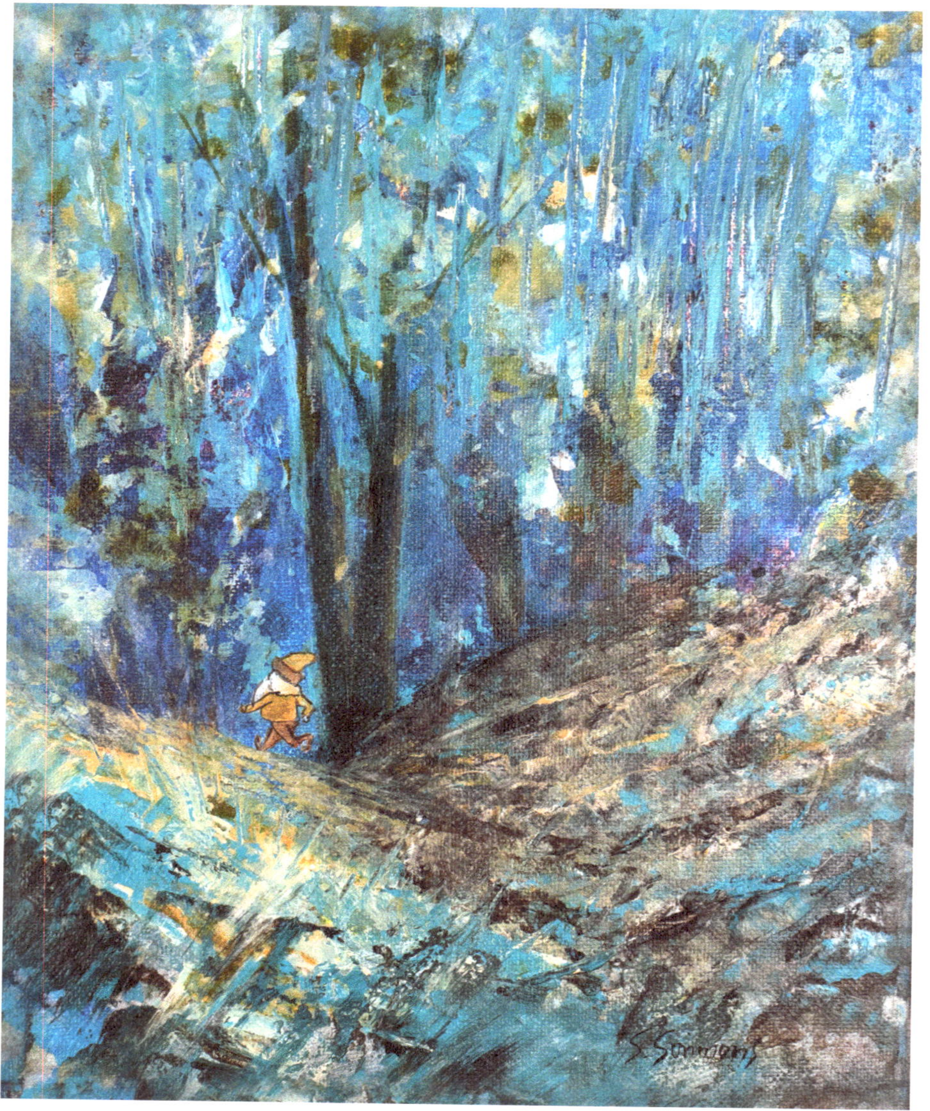

A Gnome in the Woods, 2022
Acrylic on canvas, 8" x 10"

Haiku!

Secrets in the breeze

Dancing among the branches

Reveal their ancient stories

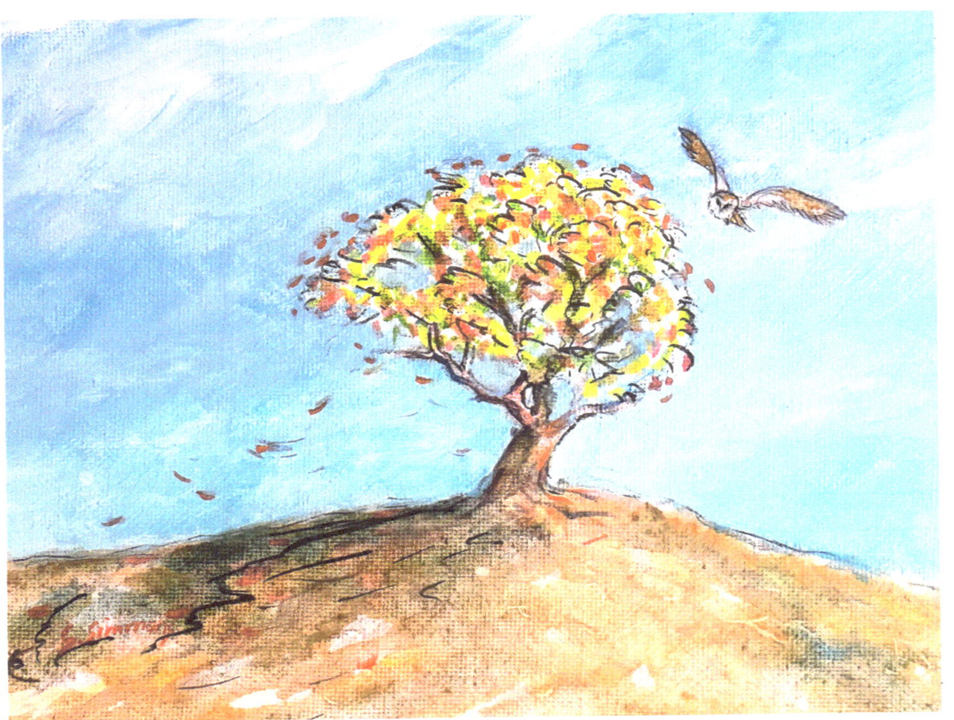

Awaken (above), 2018

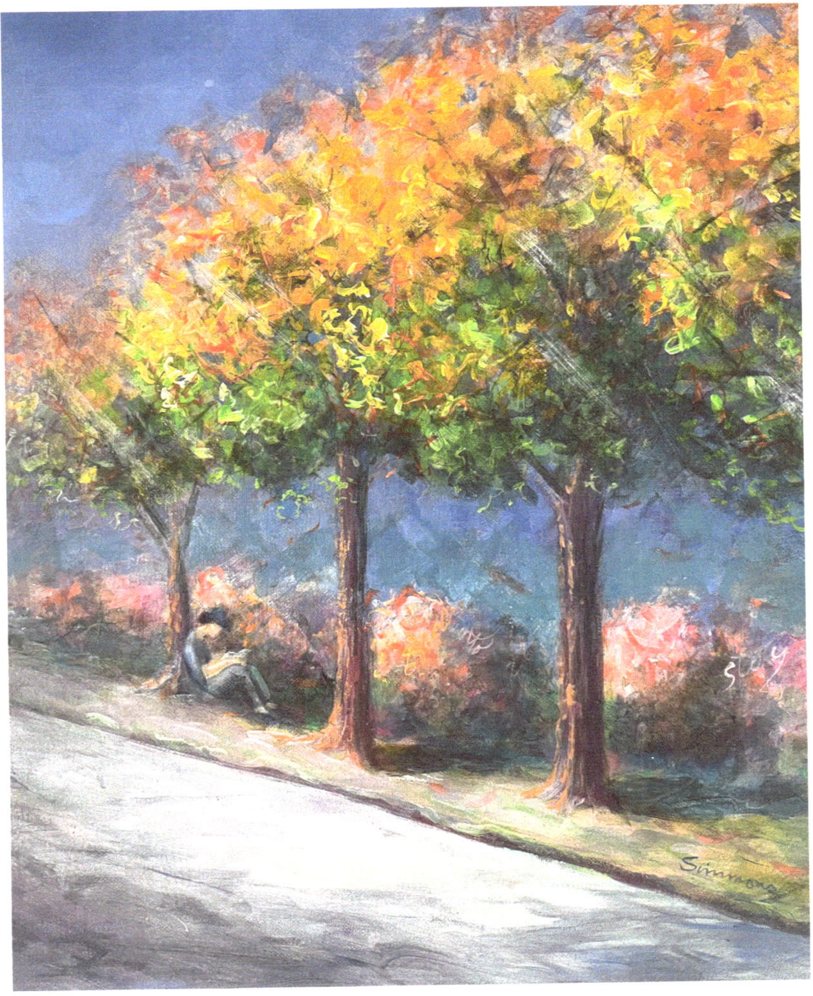

Stronger than my experiences

Lost in my own thought

New realities unfold

Awaken (above), 2018
Acrylic on canvas, 5" x 7"

Fell into a Story (right), 2020
Acrylic on canvas, 12"x 18"

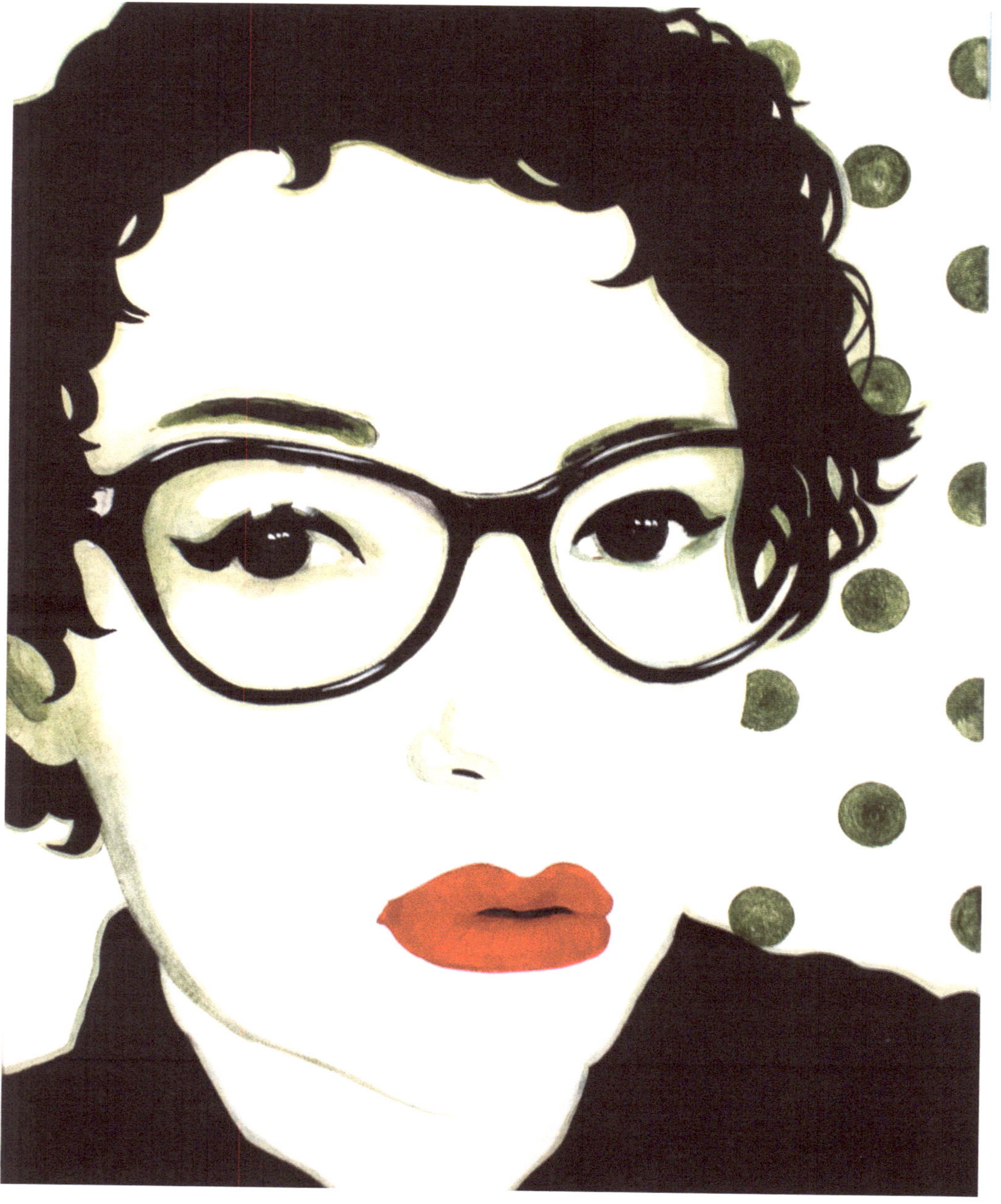

Margaret, 2022
Acrylic on canvas, 18" x 24"

Oftentimes, a dream it seems
This planet I call home
Traveling around the sun
I'm not so all alone

I see others on the bus
Going the same way
Round and round we go together
'Til we leave one day

What a perfect place to play
And visit for a while
The time we're given is a gift
I celebrate it all!

A Time to Play!

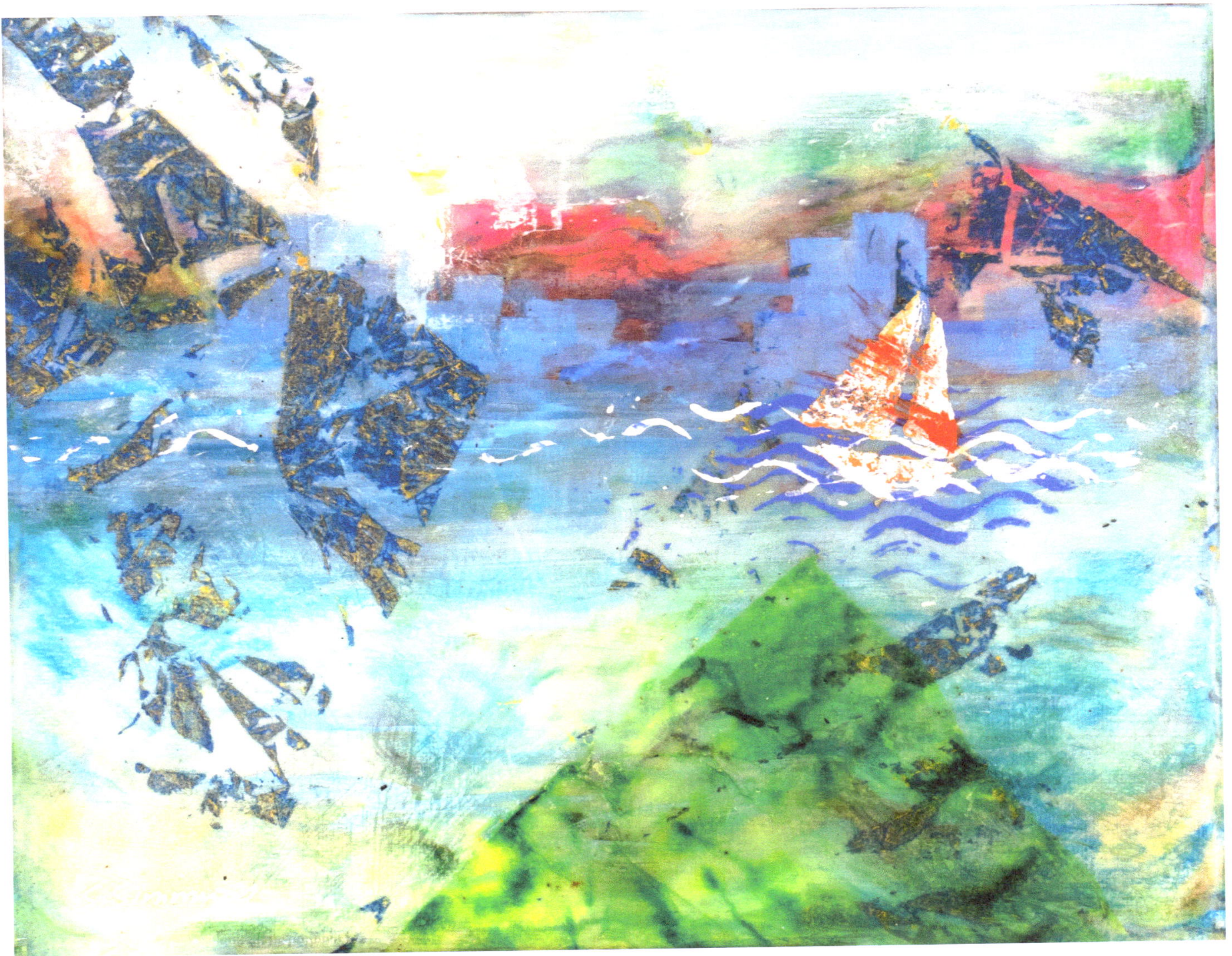

Sailing, 2022
Acrylic on canvas, 8" x 10"

Gratitude is...

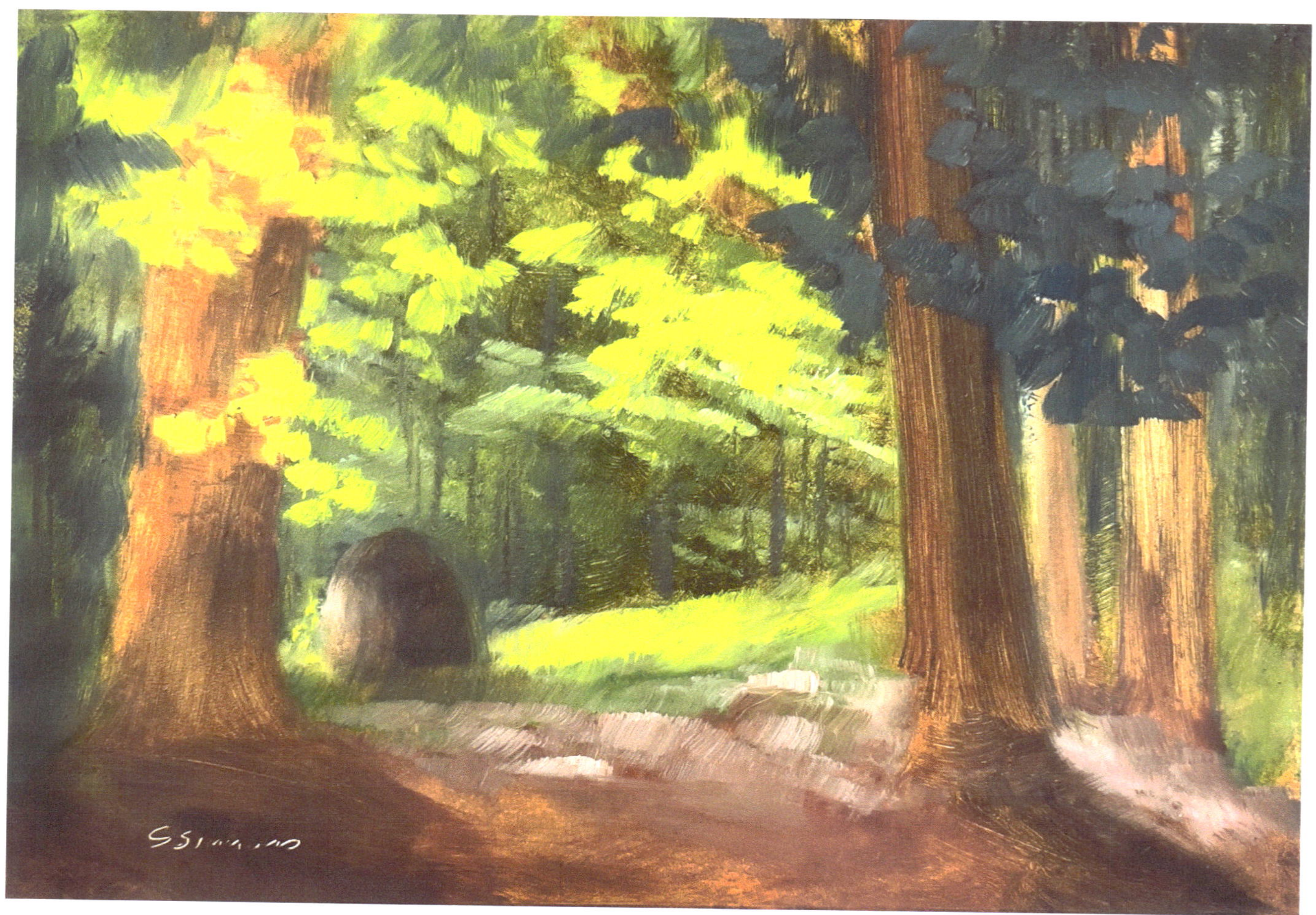

A Little Splash of Light!

*Little Splash of Light,*2025, Oil on hardboard, 5" x 7"

About the Author

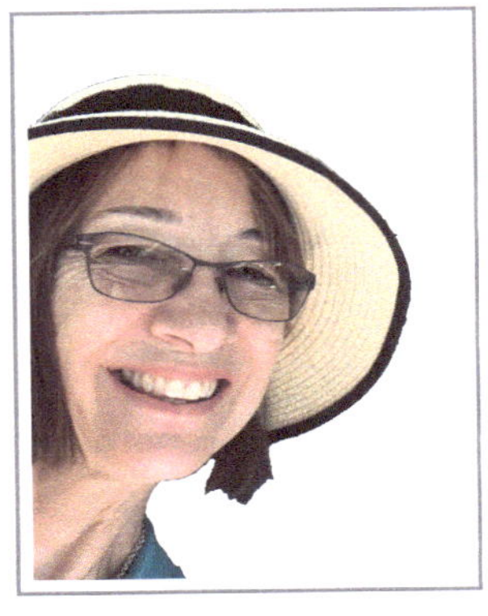

Susan Simmons of Jamestown, New York, enjoys all forms of art, including painting, sculpture, printmaking, digital art, and graphic design. The work featured in this book includes landscapes, figure, and abstract paintings in oil, acrylic, and watercolor. She is a member of North Shore Arts Alliance since 2020, and featured her first solo show at the Octagon Gallery at the Patterson Library in Westfield, New York.

Because her mother was an artist, her passion for art started at a very early age. Encouraged by her grandmother, Susan attended the University of Texas at Austin where she earned her Bachelor of Fine Arts degree in 1978. Since then, Susan has taught a variety of classes, including painting and sculpture.

Susan participates annually in the Roger Tory Peterson Institute Plein Air festival and the Jamestown ArtScape project.

Susan continues to enjoy the arts, creating imaginative, inspirational artwork for herself and her collectors.